WHISTLE PIG   COLUMBIA LIVE STAGE   THE DODGERS   and MICHAEL WATT

THE ARACA GROUP   LEN BLAVATNIK   BURNT UMBER PRODUCTIONS   MICHAEL COPPEL   KEN DAVENPORT   STEPHEN FOUND   GREENLEAF PRODUCTIONS
DAVID HARRIS   INDEPENDENT PRESENTERS NETWORK   THE JOHN GORE ORGANIZATION   STEPHANIE P. McCLELLAND
JUST FOR LAUGHS THEATRICALS/GLASS HALF FULL PRODUCTIONS   MARION ALDEN BADWAY   MARRINER GROUP
TOMMY MOTTOLA   NEDERLANDER PRESENTATIONS INC   DARYL ROTH   SONIA FRIEDMAN PRODUCTIONS
THEATER MOGUL   TULBART   DAVID WALSH   TONY & MAUREEN WHEELER
and JUJAMCYN THEATRES

present

T0081902

THE MUSICAL

Book By   Music and Lyrics by
DANNY RUBIN   TIM MINCHIN

Starring
ANDY KARL
BARRETT DOSS

with

REBECCA FAULKENBERRY   JOHN SANDERS   ANDREW CALL   RAYMOND J. LEE
HEATHER AYERS   KEVIN BERNARD   GERARD CANONICO   RHEAUME CRENSHAW   MICHAEL FATICA   KATY GERAGHTY
CAMDEN GONZALES   JORDAN GRUBB   TAYLOR IMAN JONES   TARI KELLY   JOSH LAMON   JOSEPH MEDEIROS
SEAN MONTGOMERY   WILLIAM PARRY   JENNA RUBAII   VISHAL VAIDYA   TRAVIS WALDSCHMIDT   NATALIE WISDOM

Produced for Whistle Pig by   Produced for Columbia Live Stage by   Produced for The Dodgers by
MATTHEW WARCHUS   LIA VOLLACK   MICHAEL DAVID
ANDRÉ PTASZYNSKI

Production Stage Manager   Associate Director   Associate Choreographer   Associate Directors (UK)
DAVID LOBER   THOMAS CARUSO   KATE DUNN   KATY RUDD
                                                                                    PAUL WARWICK GRIFFIN

Advertising/Marketing/Digital   Press Representative   Production Management   General Management
AKA   BONEAU/BRYAN-BROWN   AURORA PRODUCTIONS   BESPOKE THEATRICALS

Music Director   Vocal Arrangements   Music Coordinator
DAVID HOLCENBERG   TIM MINCHIN   HOWARD JOINES
                    CHRISTOPHER NIGHTINGALE

Video Design   Additional Movement   Hair, Wig & Make-Up Design   Casting
ANDRZEJ GOULDING   FINN CALDWELL   CAMPBELL YOUNG ASSOCIATES   JIM CARNAHAN, C.S.A.

Sound Design   Lighting Design   Illusions
SIMON BAKER   HUGH VANSTONE   PAUL KIEVE

Music Supervision, Orchestrations & Dance Arrangements
CHRISTOPHER NIGHTINGALE

Scenic & Costume Design
ROB HOWELL

Co-Choreographer
ELLEN KANE

Choreographed by
PETER DARLING

Directed by
MATTHEW WARCHUS

ISBN: 978-1-5400-3621-6

Visit Hal Leonard Online at
www.halleonard.com

Contact us:
Hal Leonard
7777 West Bluemound Road
Milwaukee, WI 53213
Email: info@halleonard.com

In Europe, contact:
Hal Leonard Europe Limited
42 Wigmore Street
Marylebone, London, W1U 2RN
Email: info@halleonardeurope.com

In Australia, contact:
Hal Leonard Australia Pty. Ltd.
4 Lentara Court
Cheltenham, Victoria, 3192 Australia
Email: info@halleonard.com.au

FOREWORD

Writing this musical with Danny Rubin, Matthew Warchus and Chris Nightingale was a joyous, existential adventure. There was so much that made my brain fizz when I first started to think about how we might put *Groundhog Day* on a stage.

First, I was inspired by the simple, poetic idea of a life being reflected in a day. Our musical leans on this metaphor, opening in the pre-dawn with a song which itself starts with a birth. The idea of being born at "sunrise on a sunless day" suggests a dark day, a portent of the struggle we're about to witness. But in that opening song, there is already an answer for Phil Connors, had he the wisdom to listen. The lyrics, like the town itself, are simple and pretty and folksy, but remind us that human happiness requires a level of acquiescence, an understanding that we are not all-powerful, and that despite our desire to "will the clouds away," only time will reveal the sun.

"There Will Be Sun" also immediately begins to play with ideas of circularity—musically, not just lyrically. The harmonic movement of the chorus is built on a simple climb up the major scale, resolving, like a day, in the same place it began.

In western music, an octave has twelve semitones, like the twelve hours of a clock. I obsessed over exploiting this coincidence, eventually finding expression for it in "Philanthropy" (an instrumental not included in this book). I also played with the idea of infinity in the musical's main theme which is based, you'll notice, on the harmonic movement of "Hope," and is designed to give one the sense that it might just move ever upwards. This theme begins the "Overture" and recurs at the other end of the show, in the resolution of "Seeing You": a musical sunrise and sunset.

Not only is a life like a day, it is also—as Shakespeare among others pointed out—like a play. Which is convenient. Throughout the piece we flirt with the idea that Phil Connors is not only a man trapped in his life, and not only a man who is subsequently trapped in a *day*, but he's also a player who is trapped in a *play*. And of all things, he's trapped in a bloody musical! The townspeople of Punxsutawney are initially a rather grating musical-theatre chorus, asserting their relentless positivity in a repetitive, chintzy refrain: "Punxsutawney is a little town with a heart as big as any small town in the USA," they squawk, to Phil's grimacing chagrin. On this level, Phil's journey is to find the beauty in the "musical of his life." (We were careful not to lean too hard on this *meta*-aspect, but I love that it shimmers away in the background. There are lyrics that allow you to think about the piece in this way, should you want to go searching!)

Another conceptual foundation of this score was the idea that the whole piece should echo the way our musical tastes change as we travel through our lifetimes, maturing with experience. As Phil Connors lives through the thousands of repetitions of his day-from-hell (or, metaphorically, as he travels through the various life-phases towards wisdom and eventual release), he undergoes trials which alter his emotional state. As a result, I let the style of music travel with him.

His opening number has a lyrical, melodic and rhythmic complexity that speaks to his urbane arrogance. His song is cynical and competitive, the melody angular and the lyrics intricate, with barely a breath to allow space for the world to get a word in. The cheery town has to crash in with a frickin' marching band to even have a hope of penetrating his egotism.

Then, when he finally realizes he's genuinely trapped, we are suddenly thrust into that much underutilized musical genre: Telephone Hold Music. "Stuck" is suddenly finding yourself in purgatory: a twee, '80s-keyboard-drum-machine Rumba that never resolves to the tonic. We are musically "Stuck" in a seemingly perpetual, cheesy-dentist-waiting-room loop, while our various quacks and vets offer useless solutions.

Phil's subsequent booze-fueled anarchic phase is represented by the fast and furious drunken Bluegrass of "Nobody Cares," while his sexually exploitative phase ("Philandering", an instrumental not included in this book) draws musically from the trope of '70s slap-bass, soft-porn funk!

Rita's state of mind is also reflected in stylistic choices: "One Day" has the hopeful octave jump of "Over the Rainbow," before it quickly becomes more bluesily cynical. (I always thought "blues" needed an adverb... now it does.)

When, at the top of Act II, Phil decides to end it all for both himself and his beaver-ish namesake, we fall towards shameless teen-angst-rock. This is a dark time in poor Phil's life, and as his lyric mocks the very notion of "Hope," our score takes an ironic jab at his melodramatic self-loathing. (Hopefully it works both ironically *and* *un*-ironically... after all, this was a character originally made famous by an actor who has managed to have his ironic cake and sincerely eat it too for decades!)

When Phil finally has no hope left at all (not even of successfully ending his life), sitting in the snow in a post-suicidal, nihilistic stupor, he finally tells Rita the truth about his love for her. It is the first time we have seen him be truly honest, the first time he isn't motivated by selfishness. For that reason, "Everything About You" is musically honest, introducing the simple chord movement that later develops into "Seeing You." (For lyrics nerds, note that he asserts that he knows *everything* in this song, and that he knows *nothing* in "Seeing You." Wisdom is often said to come with an acceptance of your ignorance as well as your powerlessness.)

Rita pulls Phil from the pit of despair with an uplifting, innocent pop number that exploits the most utilized chord progression of all time. (Check out The Axis of Awesome's "Four Chord Song" if you don't know what I'm talking about!) It explores the old lament, "If I had my time again..." from a new angle: what if you *literally* could live your life over? What mistakes would you rectify? What missed opportunities would you grab? Of course, Rita's natural optimism and kindness forces Phil to think a lot about his historically cynical, exploitative choices.

So Phil, taking Rita's advice, starts to try to use his time for good. He begins to learn the piano (*repetition, repetition, repetition*) and, as the endless months of Groundhog Days roll by, he begins to become a master of his little universe. But just as he's starting to find some peace in helping others and in self-improvement, he slips into despair again when he realizes he can't save the life of Old Jensen, a homeless man he's come to care for.

Enter Ned Ryerson. Previously the most annoying of the gratingly-annoying townspeople, he reveals himself to hold great wisdom born of great grief. "Night Will Come" exploits the same harmonic movement as "Hope," but keeps it a little bit more in the minor mode. It still has that sense of circularity, and thematically it is related to the simple truth of "There Will Be Sun," leaning again on the central life-as-a-day metaphor. But Ned's song is not about patiently waiting for the sun to come out; it's about acknowledging the inevitability of its going down. To really *love life*, he seems to tell us, you have to face the inevitability of death.

And so Phil enters a phase of his life in which he seeks meaning in virtuosity. His days are perfectly timed, impossibly intricate, and dedicated to helping others... and becoming a masterful musician. We tried to represent this in music, with the masterful Chris Nightingale helping me turn my flamboyant idiocy into a brilliantly orchestrated and deeply complex instrumental score. If you've bought this songbook, you've probably already got the album—thanks!—so you don't need me to tell you how good Nightingale is.

But Phil has one more step to take. And I, musically, needed to land somewhere peaceful, authentic and centered. Around the time I was writing this score, I was listening to a lot of fantastic, rootsy Americana, and although I can't pretend to be an artist with that heritage, I wanted to let myself be influenced by it. And, given this is a story about a man who begins with utter contempt for small-town rural America, it made sense to me that when he finally found true peace—when he finally realized that this place, this day, this life was *enough*—that it should sound a little like rural America. Or at least, that this urban Australian composer should let Americana have its influence.

"Seeing You" tries to bring it all together. It is the natural conclusion of the musical journey. It lands—hopefully not too heavily—on the central idea that Mr. Rubin buried in his amazing film script: happiness requires that you change the way you see the world, rather than constantly aspiring to materially alter it. And it ties up our metaphorical loose ends: the song is about his life journey, but when he sings "was it really only yesterday," and refers to his suicidal phase as a "storm [that] overwhelmed me sometime late this morning," he is speaking of life as a day. The lyrics even play with the notion that he is an actor stuck in a long-running musical: "I've spent a lifetime seeking signs, reading lines..." although, rather too trickily I suppose, these words also refer to his job as a meteorologist. A meteorologist is, of course, someone who spends their life trying to predict what is going to happen tomorrow.

In the middle of "Seeing You" is a huge breath of silence. If we've all done our job, the audience, like Phil, will sit happily in the beauty of the space. In inspirational, fridge-magnet terms, Phil has learned to live in the moment.

Danny Rubin is a brilliant, lovely man, who had a brilliant, lovely idea. And, man, we had fun making it into a musical.

And I dearly hope you have fun playing these selections.

Thanks for reading my ramblings. Thanks for caring about our piece.

Love and peace,
Tim
Fall, 2019

"As I say, it's a little complex"—A PERFORMANCE NOTE

On a first approach to Tim's music, a performer (and certainly transcriber) can be hit with a rhythmic curveball when tackling a sung line. Part of the individuality—and genius—of this writing is that many phrases do not line up with the meter of the accompaniment and in fact almost defy notation in their stresses and cross-rhythms. Those characters with their own set of rules, often at odds with everyone around them, now seem to have their own set of rhythmic rules. Think of *Matilda* and Miss Trunchbull's "persistently resisting this anarchistic mischiefin'"—15 syllables effortlessly in the space of 16. And this brilliant disregard for standard notation is here at its fruitiest in *Groundhog Day*.

Tim highlights in his foreword the purposeful complexity of Phil's music in "Small Town USA [Day One]." Just listen, for example, how the primarily straight-8th melodies in this number sit against primarily swung accompaniments—musically strengthening the defiance of Phil to fit in with the Punxsutawney locals. But whereas songs like "Punxsutawney Phil" and "If I Had My Time Again" are not too complex to notate, plenty of other stuff pushes the boundaries. "These endless first dates, that start with her hating me," fits yet doesn't really fit over Rita singing "One day, some day, my prince may come," as at this point these two characters are dramatically poles apart. Some cool cross-rhythms slot in nicely—"You have Satan within you, we must exorcise your demons" or "But for whose sake am I making all this effing effort for"—but some may stump, if you score-read them too literally—"An ever-lasting farcical disaster. You play your part, you march the march, you don't complain." And it's not just Phil. Why all those combinations of triplets, dotted notes, and quintuplets in Rita's diary entries? The reality, the trick to it all is, of course, straightforward: the rhythms of these moments are much closer to speech patterns than normally encountered in a book musical. These moments of over-precise notation are almost self-contradicting in fact, as they're arguably more an *indication* of the melody and amount of time taken in which to sing those lines. It is more the intention of the character in that scene which will likely inform the speed and meter. Find the actor's natural speech pattern and that's probably how best to sing it. No wonder Tim left it to someone else to write this stuff down...

Laurie Perkins, *transcription-chap of all things Minchin/Nightingale.*

OVERTURE

By TIM MINCHIN
and CHRISTOPHER NIGHTINGALE

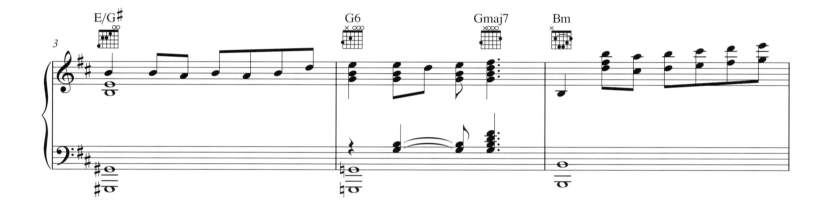

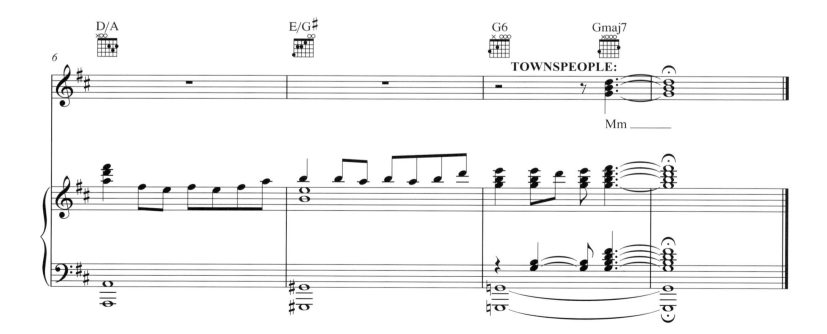

THERE WILL BE SUN

Words and Music by
TIM MINCHIN

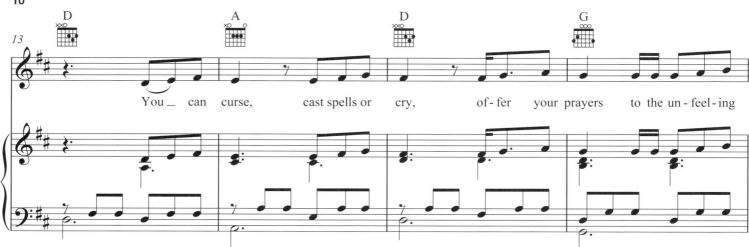

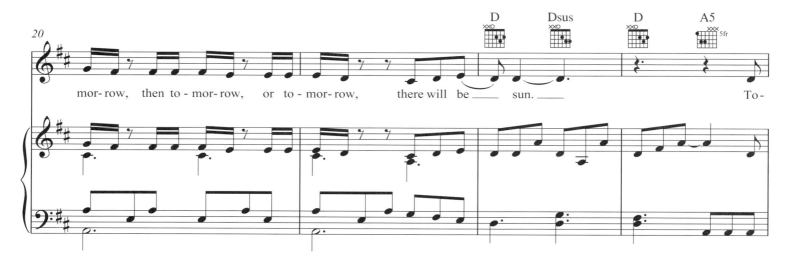

blue skies, __ my friend, bright eyes and laugh - ter. To -

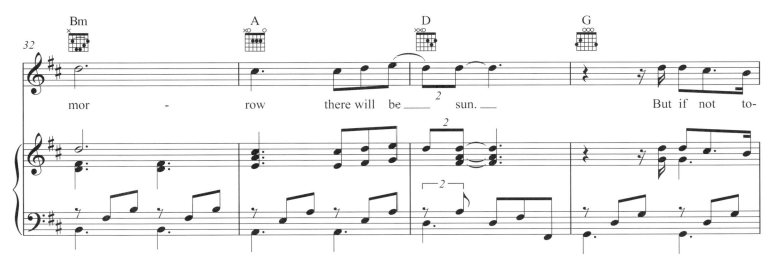

mor - row there will be _____ sun. __ But if not to-

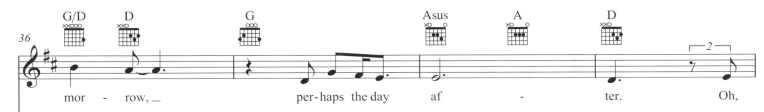

mor - row, __ per-haps the day af - ter. Oh,

if I could I'd will these clouds a - way, _____ my love. I'd

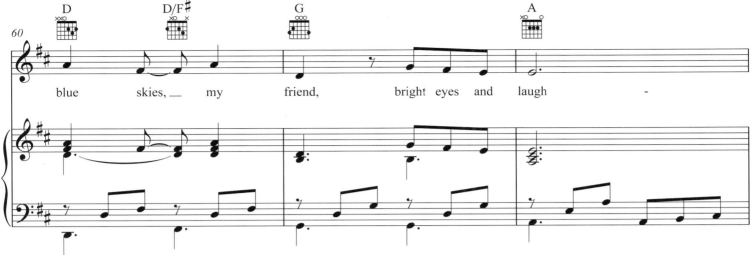

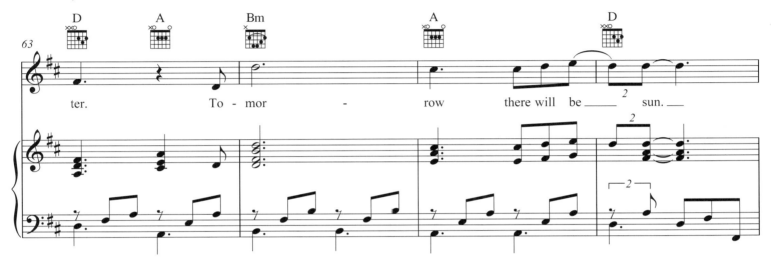

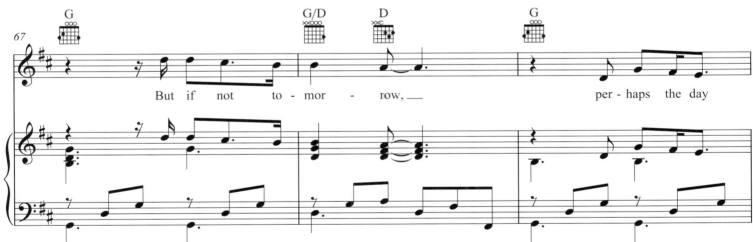

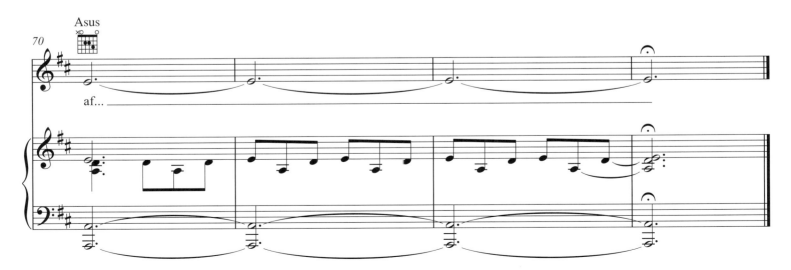

SMALL TOWN USA [DAY ONE]

Words and Music by
TIM MINCHIN

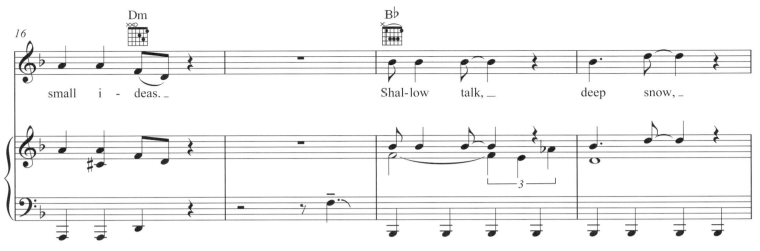

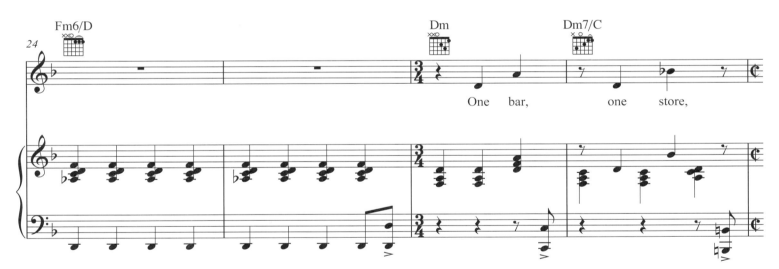

one cop.

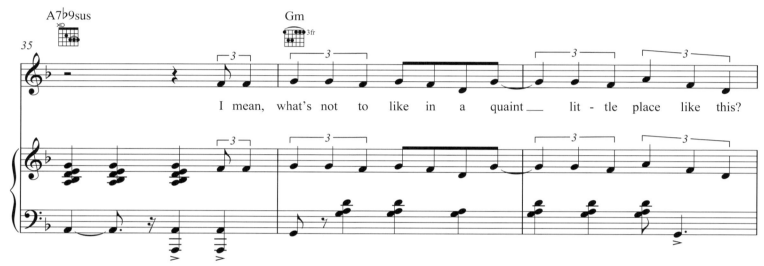

I mean, what's not to like in a quaint ___ lit - tle place like this?

Who does - n't dig a cro - cheted ___ pil - low case like this? Wa - ter col - ors of

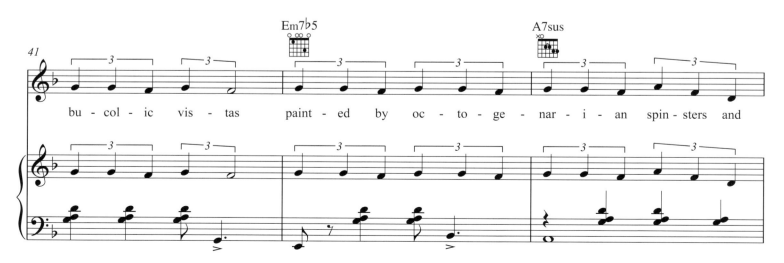

bu - col - ic vis - tas paint - ed by oc - to - ge - nar - i - an spin - sters and

all of the peo-ple just get-ting to-geth-er for re - lent-less a-nal-y-

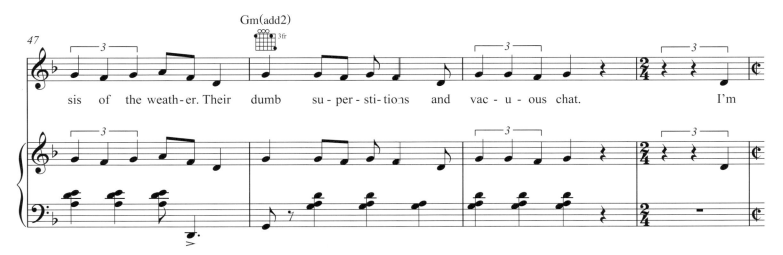

sis of the weath-er. Their dumb su-per-sti-tions and vac-u-ous chat.   I'm

sure there was a pack of Xan-ax in this jack-et.   You could-n't pay me to

stay   here   one   more   night.   Swear that there is   no   check you could write that might

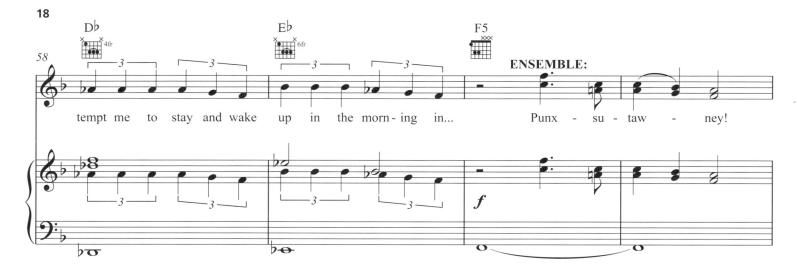

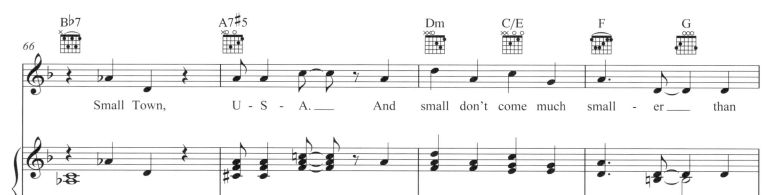

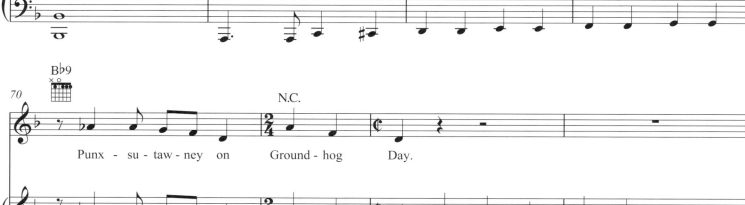

Straight 8ths

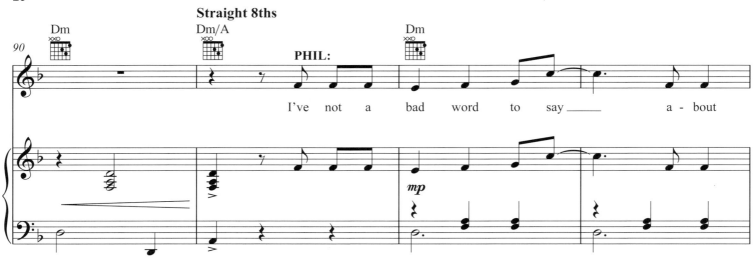

I've not a bad word to say _____ a - bout

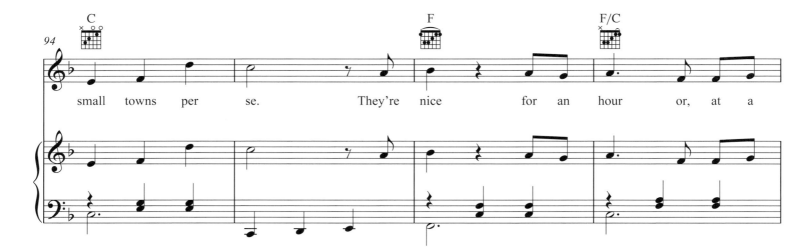

small towns per se. They're nice for an hour or, at a

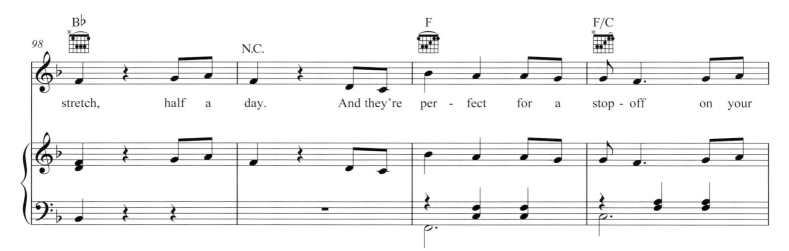

stretch, half a day. And they're per - fect for a stop - off on your

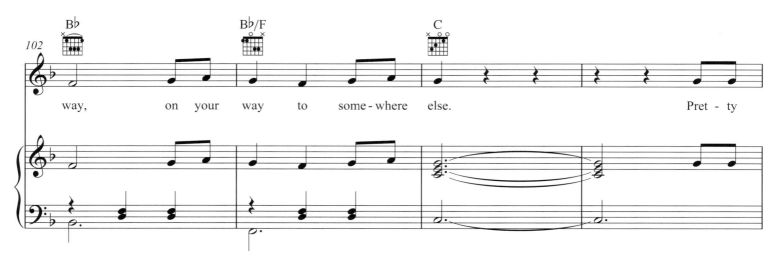

way, on your way to some - where else. Pret - ty

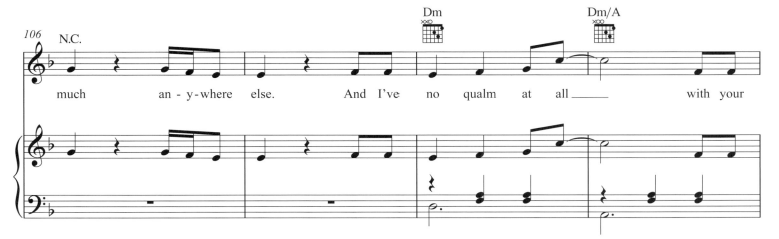

much an-y-where else. And I've no qualm at all _____ with your

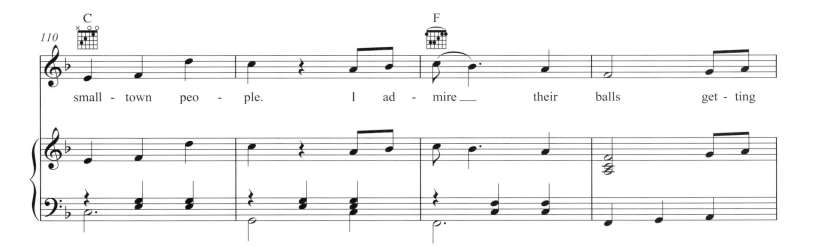

small - town peo - ple. I ad - mire _____ their balls get - ting

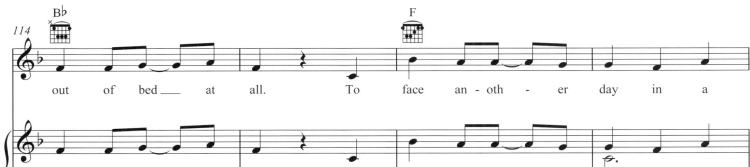

out of bed _____ at all. To face an-oth - er day in a

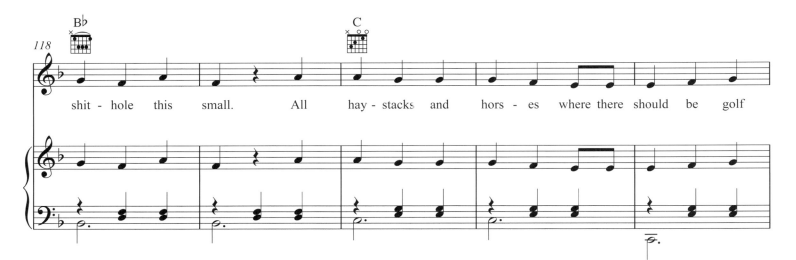

shit - hole this small. All hay - stacks and hors - es where there should be golf

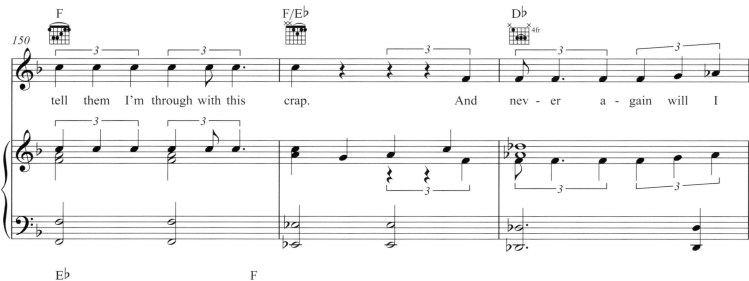

tell them I'm through with this crap. And nev-er a-gain will I

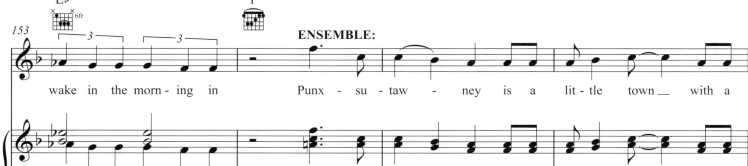

wake in the morn-ing in

ENSEMBLE:

Punx-su-taw- ney is a lit-tle town__ with a

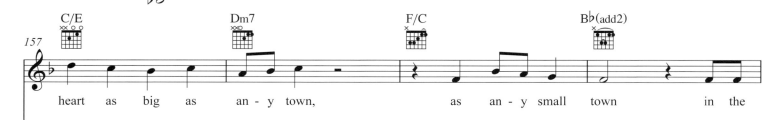

heart as big as an-y town, as an-y small town in the

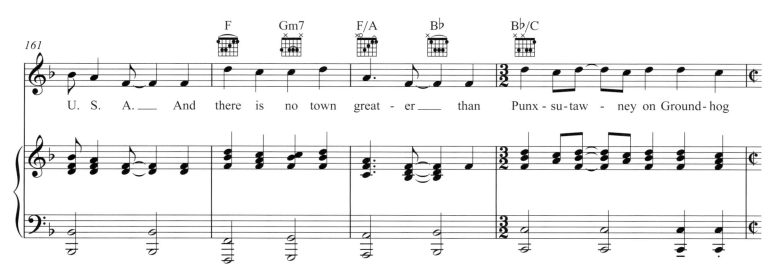

U. S. A.__ And there is no town great-er__ than Punx-su-taw - ney on Ground-hog

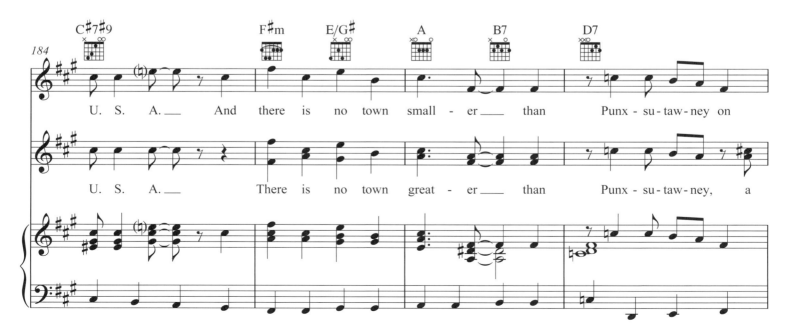

PUNXSUTAWNEY PHIL

Words and Music by
TIM MINCHIN

match this lit-tle guy's _ un-can-ny skill. We can guess, but we won't know if we should

dress for sun or snow, un-til we hear it from ol' Punx-su-taw - ney Phil!

Slower

BUSTER:

Ev-er-y year for a hun-dred years we've bent our heads and lent our ears __ to

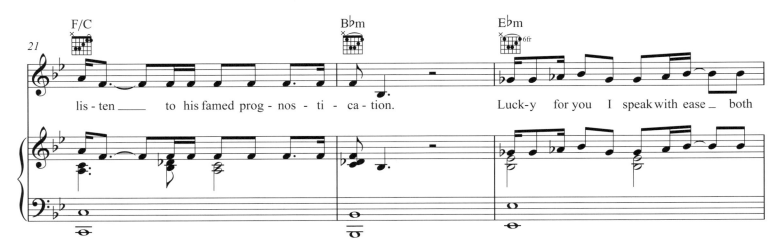

lis-ten ____ to his famed prog-nos-ti-ca-tion. Luck-y for you I speak with ease _ both

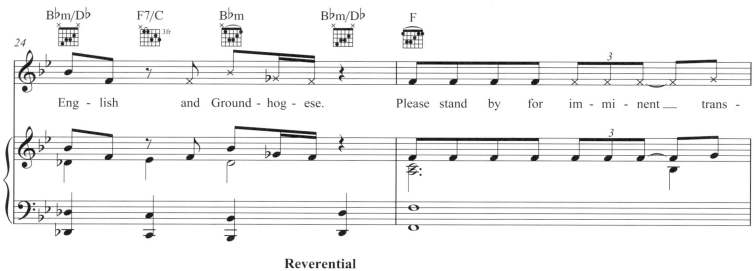

Eng - lish and Ground - hog - ese. Please stand by for im - mi - nent ___ trans -

Reverential

3 ELDERS:

la - tion. This brown log con - tain - eth ___

one ground - hog. The fa - mous ___ Phil - ip of Punx - su -

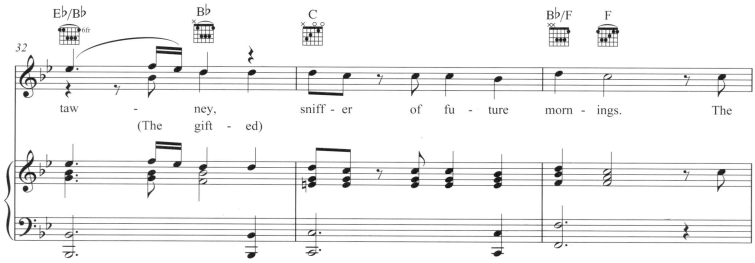

taw - ney, sniff - er of fu - ture morn - ings. The
(The gift - ed)

Sha-man of the shad-ows. Spring-er of the spring. Is it a squir-rel!? Is it a bea-ver!?

BUSTER: **ALL:**

Kind-a both, but not quite ei-ther! All the me-teor-ol-o-gists the world has ev-er known __ can-not

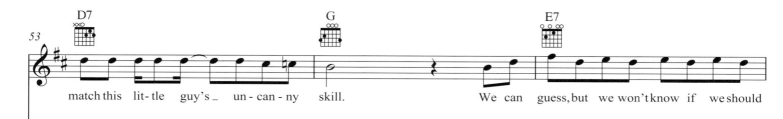

match this lit-tle guy's __ un-can-ny skill. We can guess, but we won't know if we should

dress for sun or snow un-til we hear it from ol' Punx-su-taw-ney Phil!

All the me-teor-ol-o-gists the world has ev-er known_ can-not match this lit-tle guy's_ un-can-ny

skill. We can guess, but we won't know if we should dress for sun or snow un-til we

hear it from ol' Punx-su-taw - ney Phil! _____

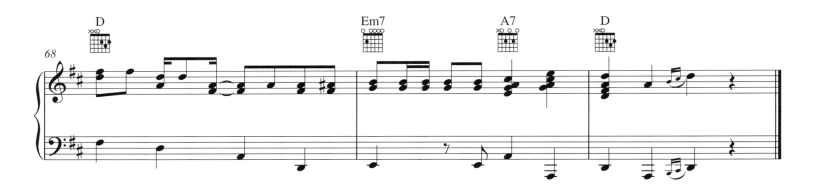

RITA'S DIARY

Words and Music by
TIM MINCHIN

Hope-ful-ly to-mor-row the roads— will be cleared and we can go mor - row there will be _____ sun.

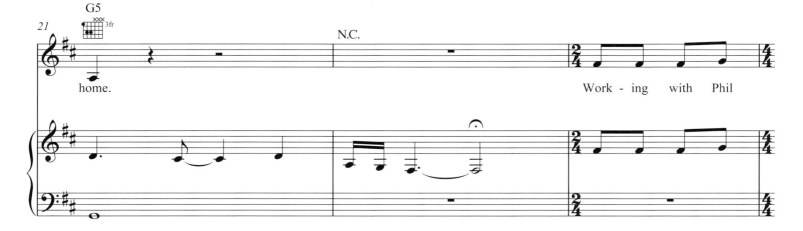

home. Work - ing with Phil

Con-nors. They all told me he would be an ass-hole. And he

ENSEMBLE A: And if not to-mor-row.

ENSEMBLE B: And if not to-mor-row.

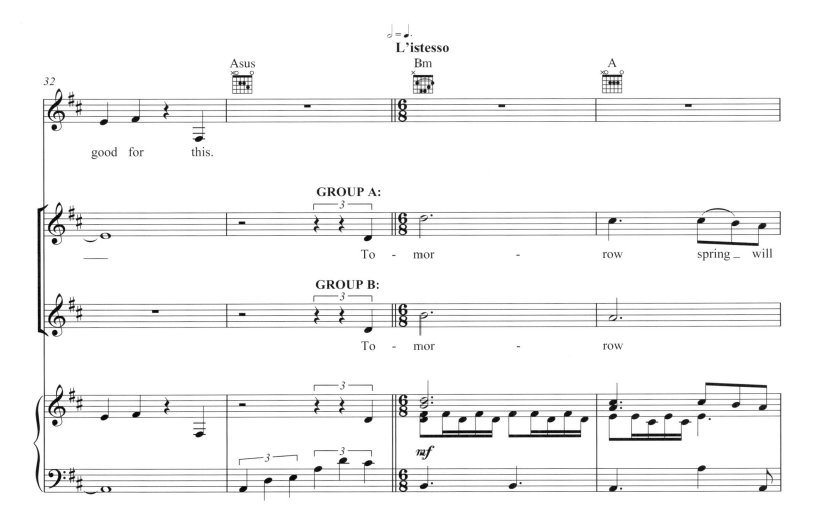

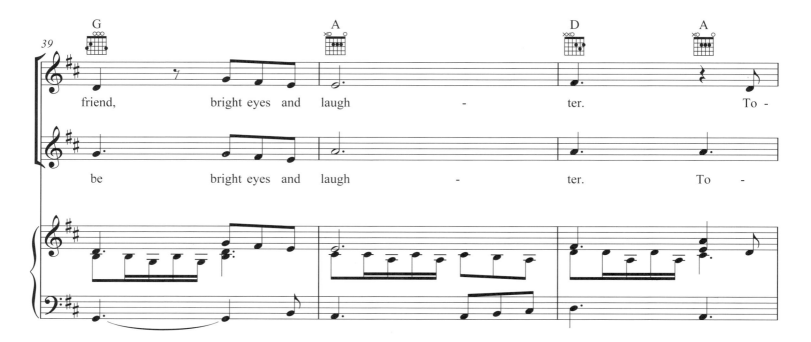

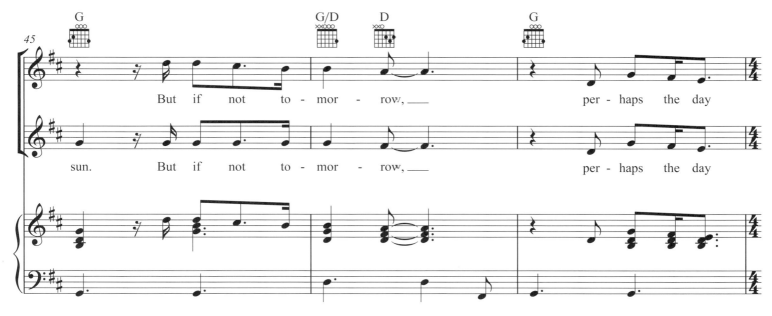

But if not to-mor - row, ____ per - haps the day

sun. But if not to-mor - row, ____ per - haps the day

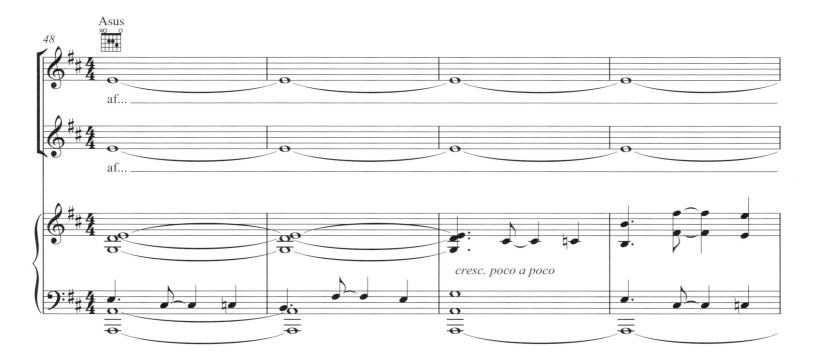

af... ____

af... ____

cresc. poco a poco

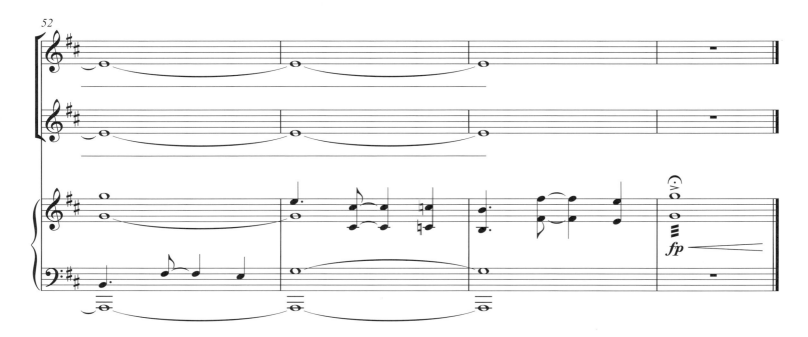

fp

SMALL TOWN USA [DAY TWO]

Words and Music by
TIM MINCHIN

Blah blah blah blah blah blah __ blah blah. You're so fired. __

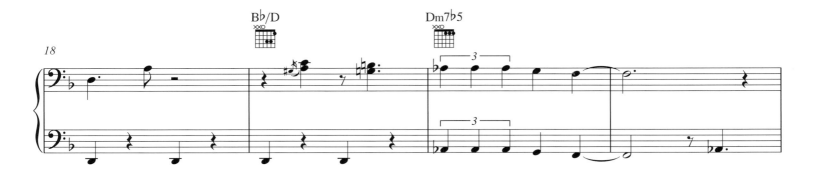

God damn am - a - teurs!

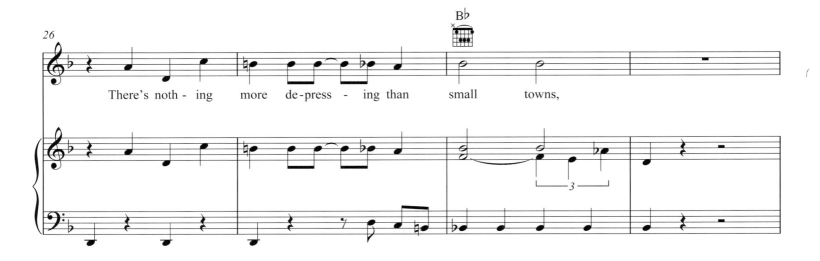

There's noth - ing more de-press - ing than small towns,

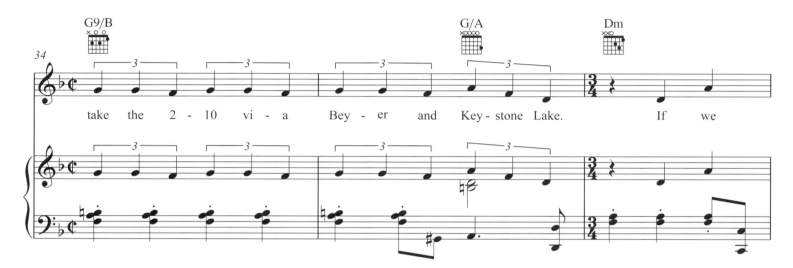

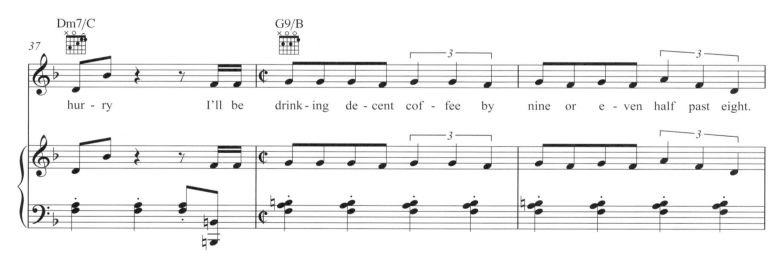

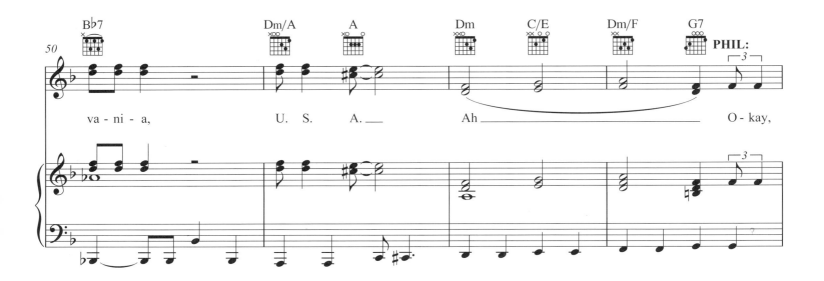

Straight 8ths

One: I'm still sleep-ing and this, I'm just dream-ing it. Two: it's a prank and

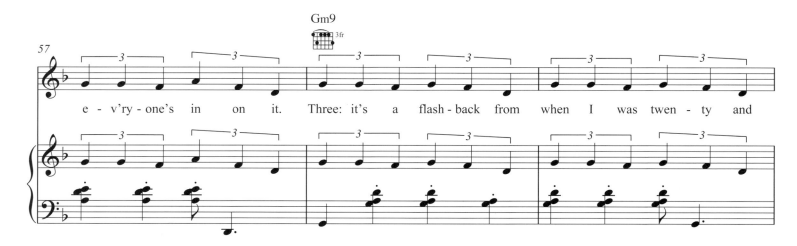

e-v'ry-one's in on it. Three: it's a flash-back from when I was twen-ty and

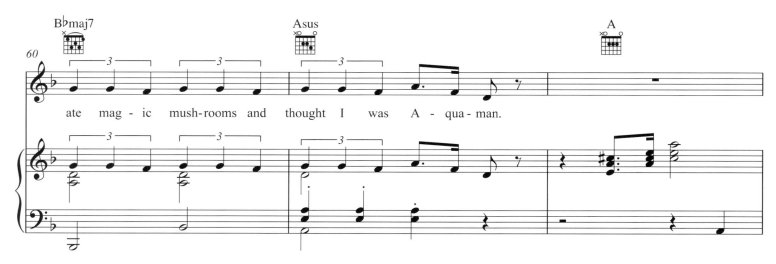

ate mag - ic mush-rooms and thought I was A - qua-man.

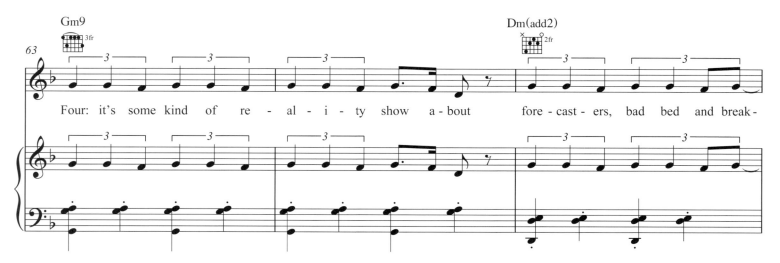

Four: it's some kind of re - al - i - ty show a - bout fore - cast - ers, bad bed and break-

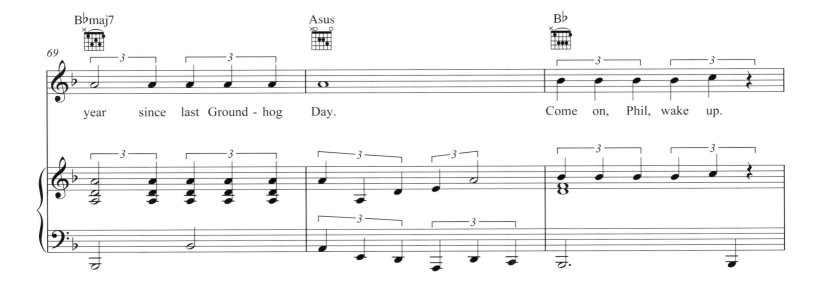

just need a mo - ment, I just need a rest.

lit - tle town ___ with a heart as big as an - y town,

as an - y small town in the U. S. A. ___ And there is no town

great - er ___ than Punx - su - taw - ney on Ground - hog... Ground - hog... Ground - hog...

STUCK

Words and Music by
TIM MINCHIN

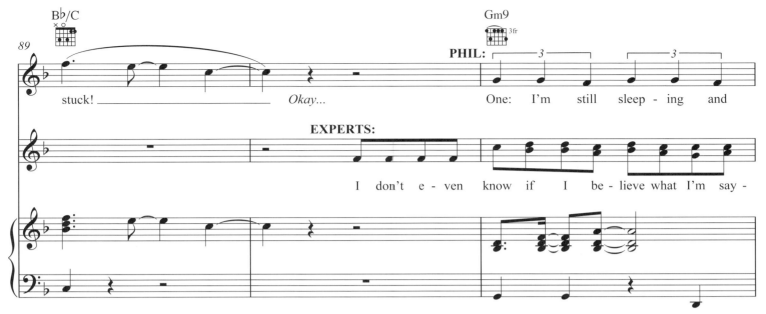

NOBODY CARES

Words and Music by TIM MINCHIN
and CHRISTOPHER NIGHTINGALE

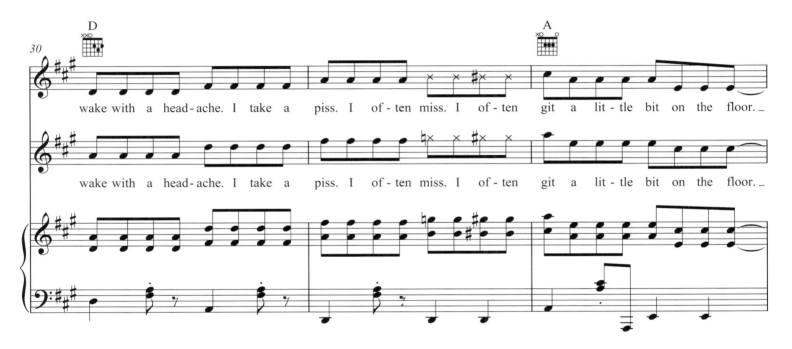

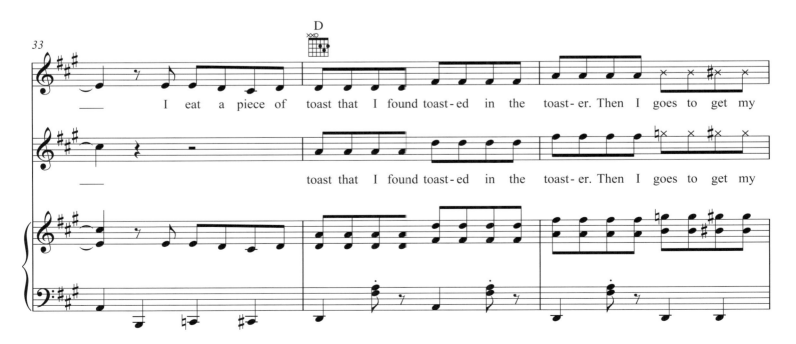

af - ter that, the bar. No - bod - y cares ___ what I

af - ter that, the bar. No - bod - y cares ___ what I

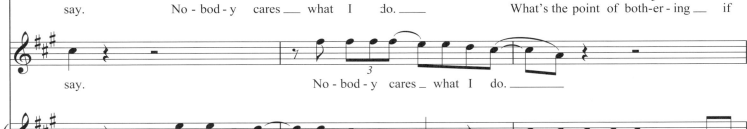

say. No - bod - y cares ___ what I do. ___ What's the point of both-er-ing ___ if

say. No - bod - y cares ___ what I do. ___

no one else is both-ered? I was born in this town ___ and I'm gon - na die ___ here,

No one else is both-ered... ...born in this town ___ and I'm gon - na die ___ here,

Fast, straight 8ths

too.

too.

RALPH:
GUS:
PHIL:

I wake with a ___ head - ache. I take a piss. ___ I of - ten

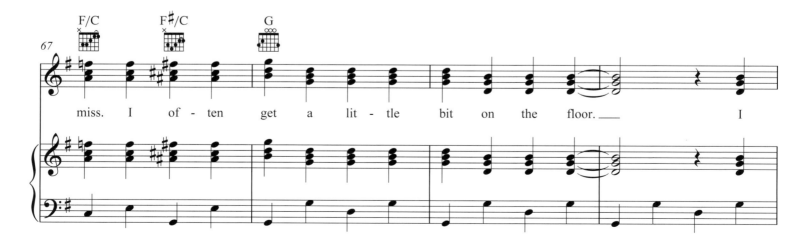

miss. I of - ten get a lit - tle bit on the floor. ___ I

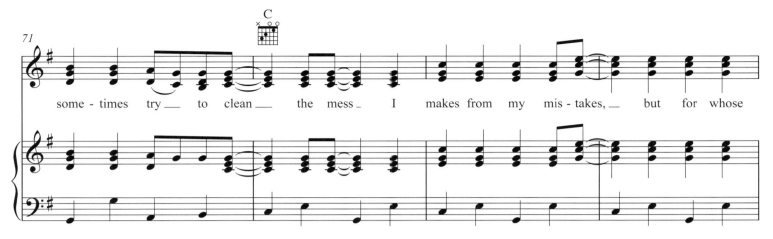

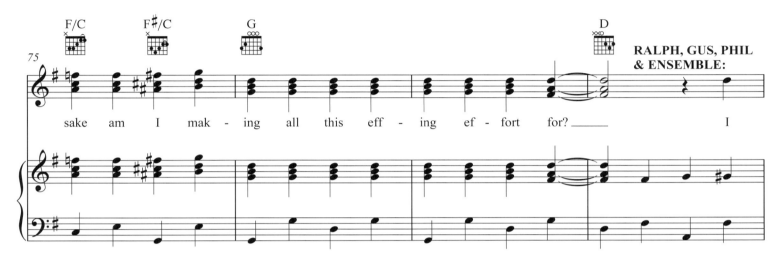

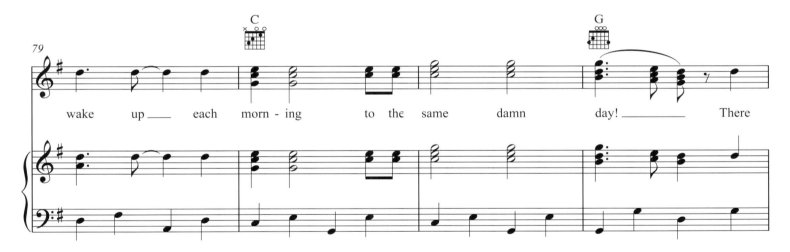

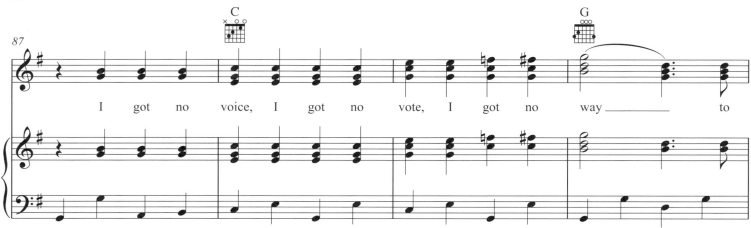

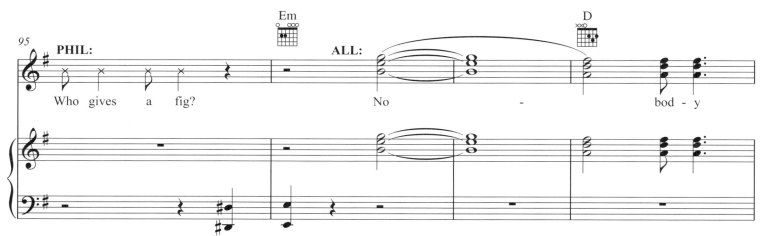

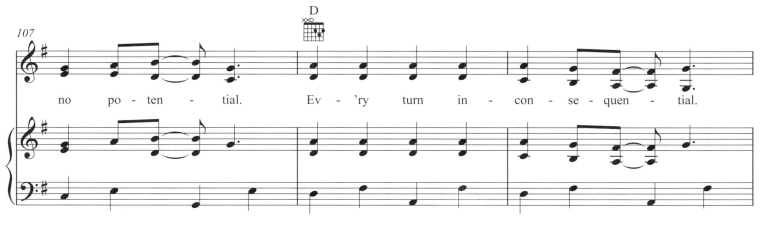

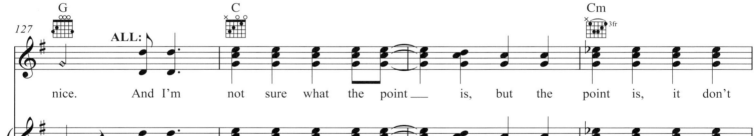

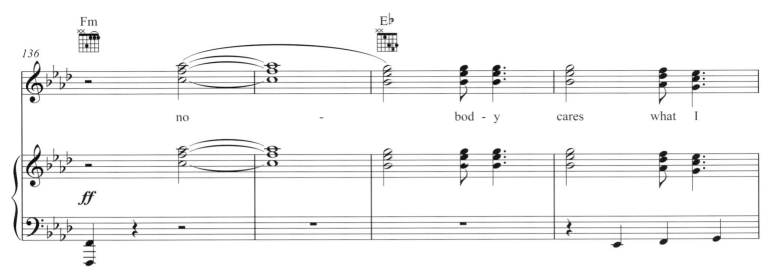

ONE DAY

Words and Music by
TIM MINCHIN

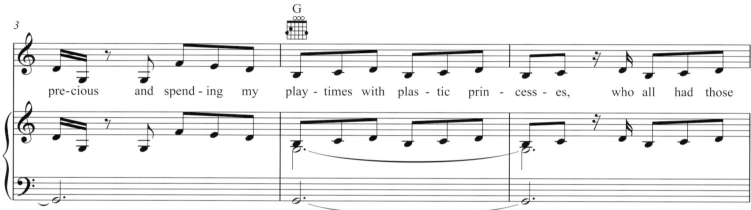

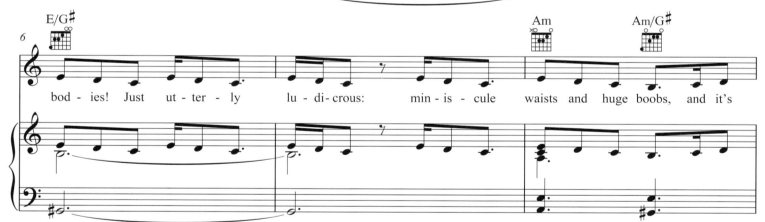

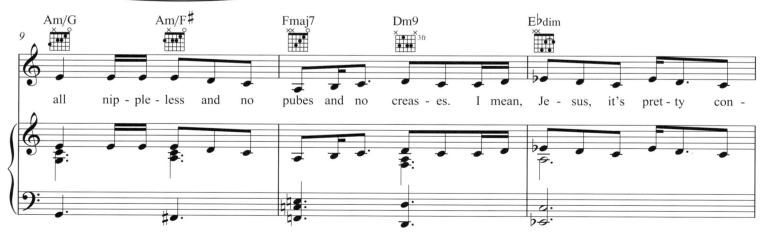

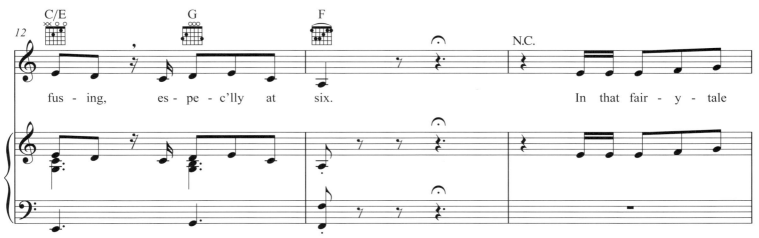

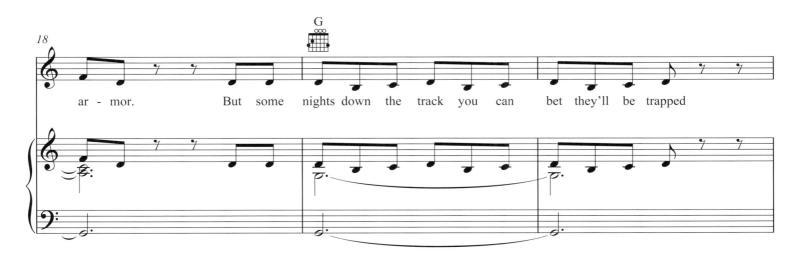

or at a ball with some har - lot. I'm not bit - ter. It's just bet - ter that I don't fall for all that

Ro - man - tic bull - shit   now that I'm old - er. Al - though I quite like the thought of being tossed

colla voce

o - ver a shoul - der, and trot - ted off to a man - sion by some rug - ged - ly hand - some man in a fire - man hel - met and

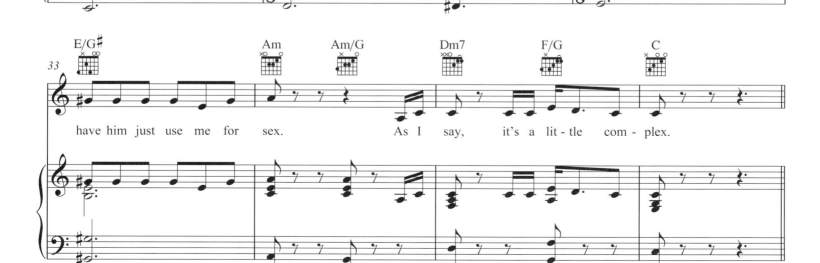

have him just use me for sex.   As I say,   it's a lit - tle com - plex.

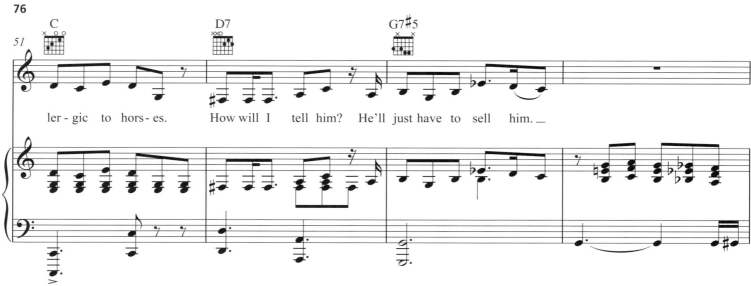

ler - gic to hors - es. How will I tell him? He'll just have to sell him. __

Brighter

I went to school with a girl, I re - mem - ber her well. She was

pret - ty smart and pret - ty as hell. Her folks had a farm, but she would - n't

Bright Latin feel

stay, of course. She want - ed Prince Charm - ing, so she went to L. A., of course. Man - aged to se -

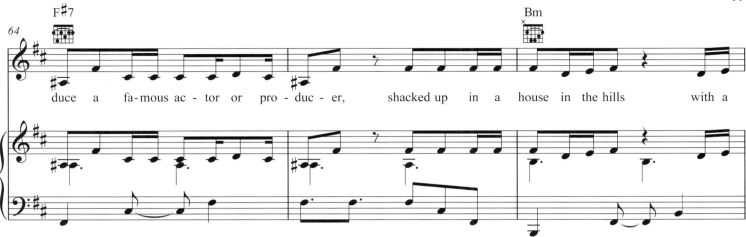

duce a fa-mous ac - tor or pro - duc - er, shacked up in a house in the hills with a

cat and a juic - er, and a fan - cy car ____ and a ten - nis court. But the guy ___

Broader, end Latin feel

___ was - n't quite the catch she thought she'd caught. He treats her like trash, and then—

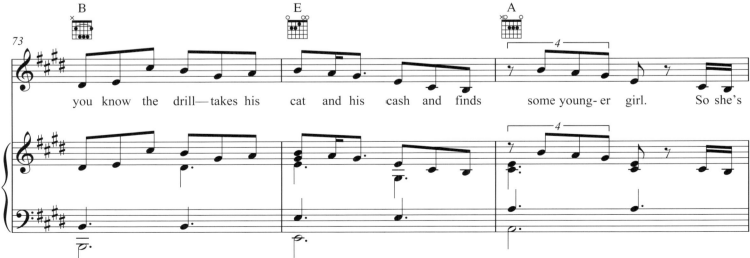

you know the drill—takes his cat and his cash and finds some young-er girl. So she's

spend the next four dec-ades want-ing to cheat on me, get-ting less hand-some and

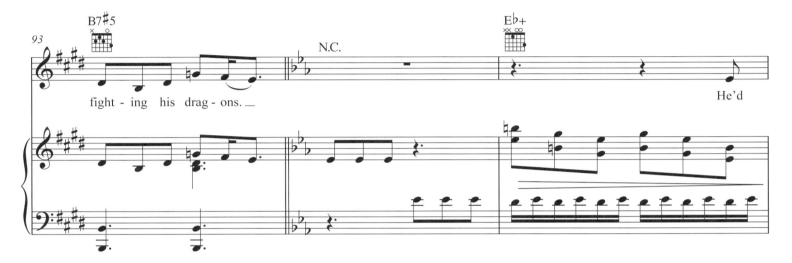

fight-ing his drag-ons. ___ He'd

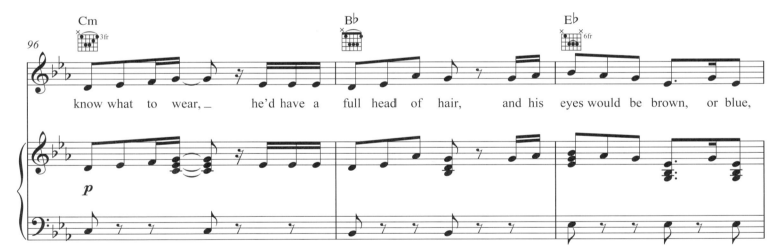

know what to wear, ___ he'd have a full head of hair, and his eyes would be brown, or blue,

or green, well I don't care. And his bod-y would be toned with those pecs like you get at the

gym. But he won't spend all his time at the gym. And he'll love read-ing books. He'll be an

ex - cel - lent cook. He'll be good - look ing but not too a - ware __ of his looks. He'll be

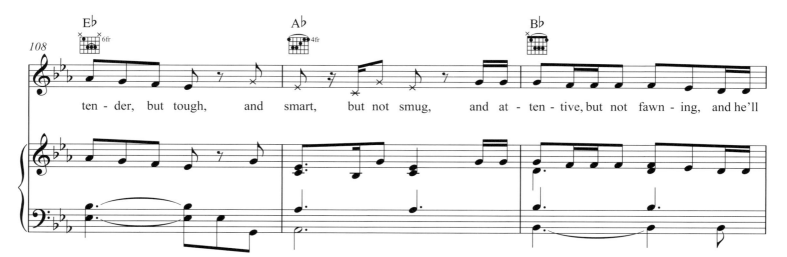

ten - der, but tough, and smart, but not smug, and at - ten - tive, but not fawn - ing, and he'll

smell good in the morn - ing, and he'll dance... *This is a guy we're talking about, right?* ...and like hik - ing and

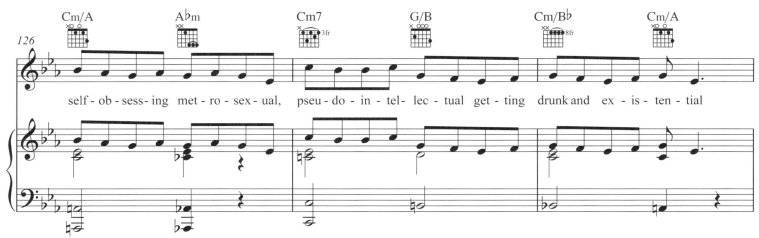

self-ob-sess-ing met-ro-sex-ual, pseu-do-in-tel-lec-tual get-ting drunk and ex-is-ten-tial

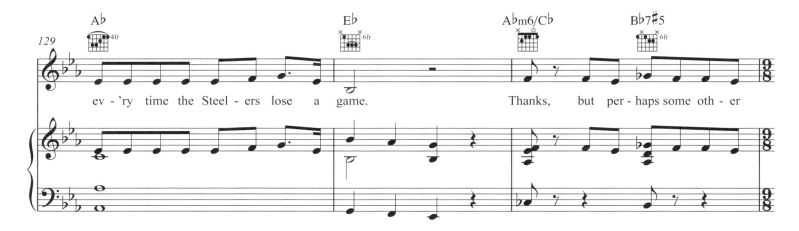

ev-'ry time the Steel-ers lose a game. Thanks, but per-haps some oth-er

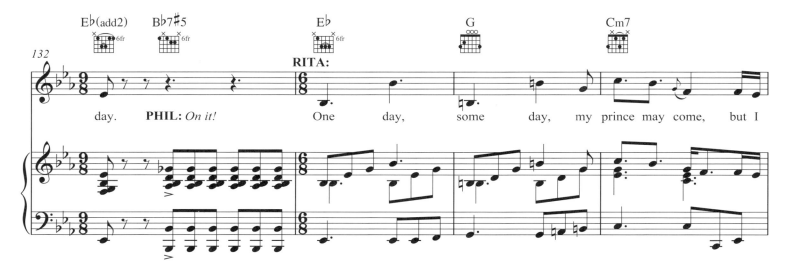

RITA:

day. **PHIL:** *On it!* One day, some day, my prince may come, but I

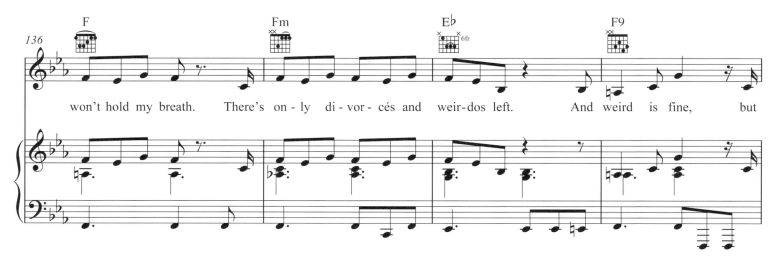

won't hold my breath. There's on-ly di-vor-cés and weir-dos left. And weird is fine, but

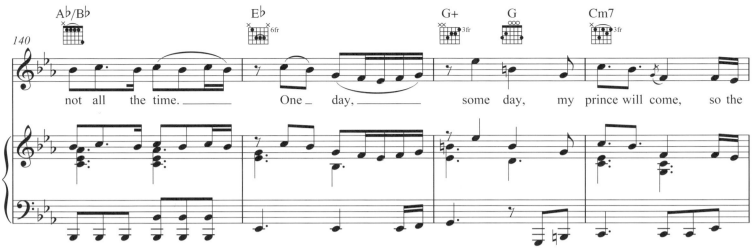

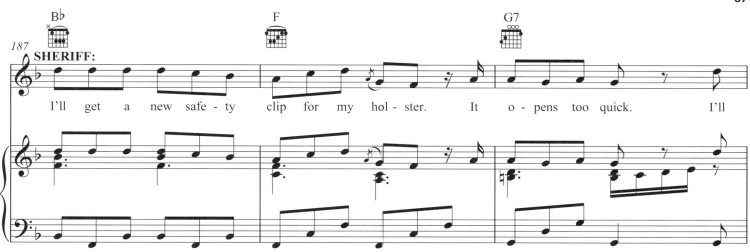

SHERIFF: I'll get a new safe-ty clip for my hol-ster. It o-pens too quick. I'll

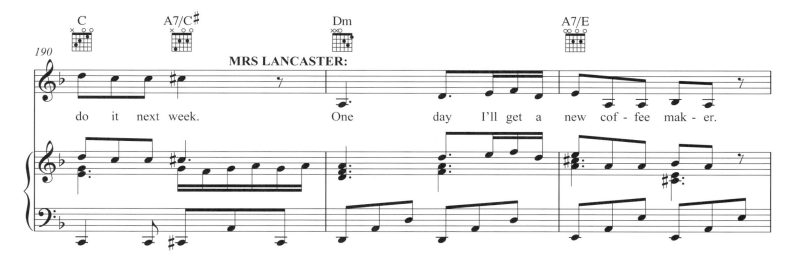

do it next week. MRS LANCASTER: One day I'll get a new cof-fee mak-er.

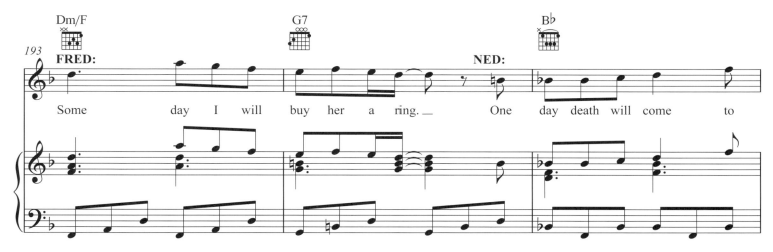

FRED: Some day I will buy her a ring. NED: One day death will come to

ev - 'ry-one. DORIS: One day I'll learn how to sing!

mor-row, and to-mor-row, and to-mor-row, and to-mor-row, and to-mor-row, and to-mor-row, and to-

mor-row, and to-mor-row, and to-mor-row, and to-mor-"rah."

Gmaj7(no3,add♭6)

(Alarm) *f cresc.*

fff

PLAYING NANCY

Words and Music by
TIM MINCHIN

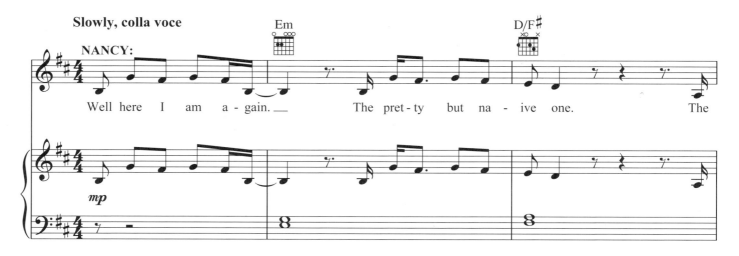

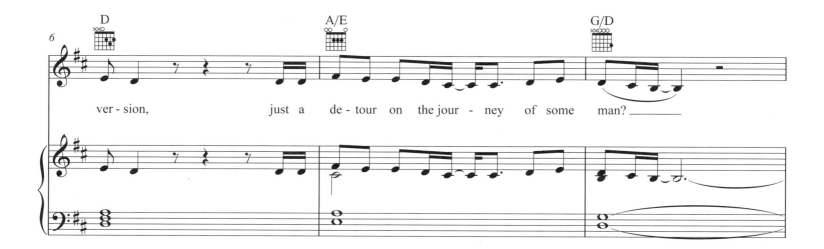

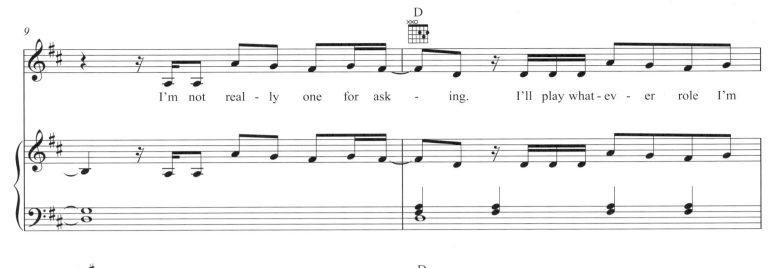

I'm not real - ly one for ask - ing. I'll play what - ev - er role I'm

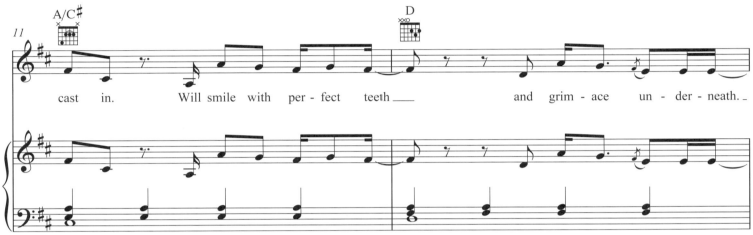

cast in. Will smile with per - fect teeth ___ and grim - ace un - der - neath. ___

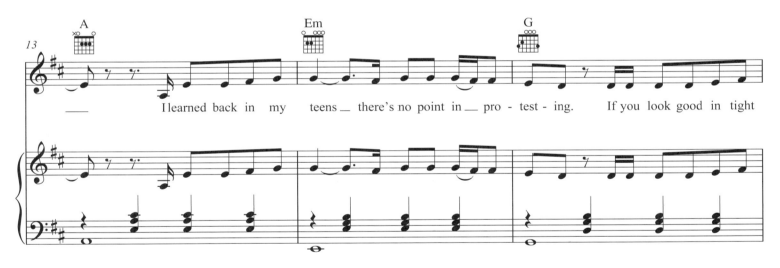

___ I learned back in my teens ___ there's no point in ___ pro - test - ing. If you look good in tight

jeans, that's what they'll want ___ you dressed in. Once you're known for low - cut

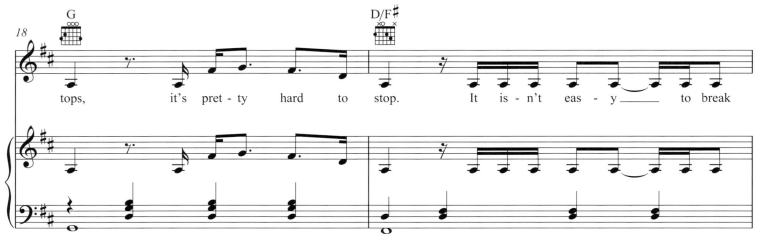

tops, it's pret-ty hard to stop. It is-n't eas-y_____ to break

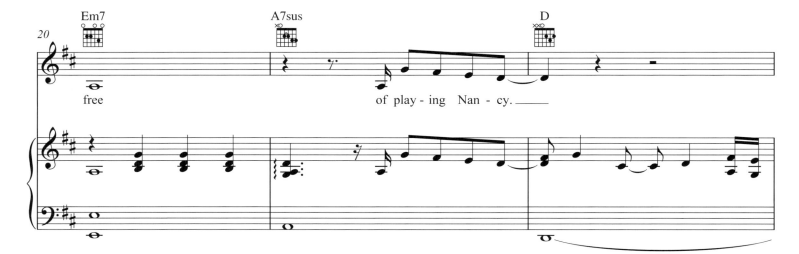

free of play-ing Nan-cy._____

I don't real-ly re-mem-ber. I guess I chose to be____ here. I was-n't quite a-ware___

____that I was put here to be stared___ at. But this world I chose___ to live___

And look, I know this per - son fits___ me. I'm pret - ty good at be - ing

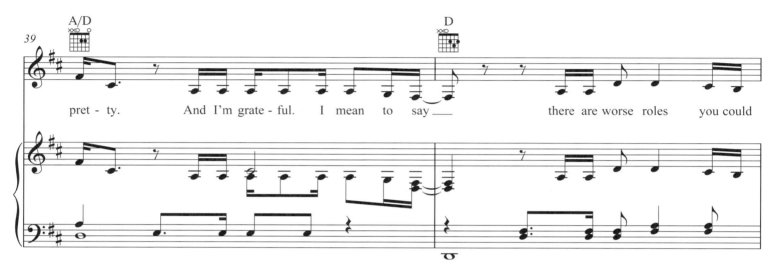

pret - ty. And I'm grate - ful. I mean to say___ there are worse roles you could

play. And I'd rath - er be___ up danc - ing than sat a - gainst___ the wall.___

___ It's bet - ter to___ be leered___ at than not de - sired___ at all.___

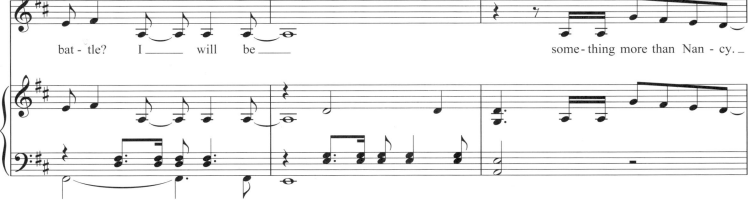

HOPE

Words and Music by
TIM MINCHIN

There will be morn - ings you'll be ut - ter - ly de - feat -

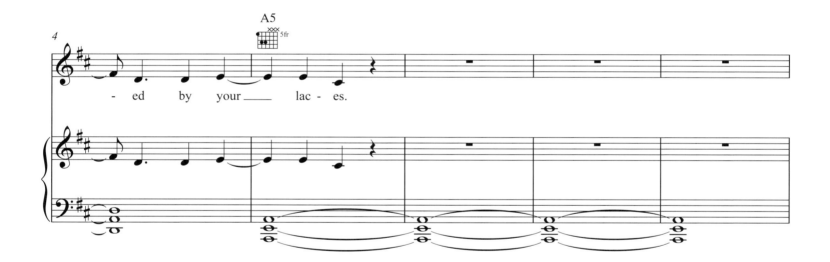

- ed by your ___ lac - es.

Days when ev - 'ry look looks con - de - scend - ing. ___ Emp - ty smiles in emp - ty

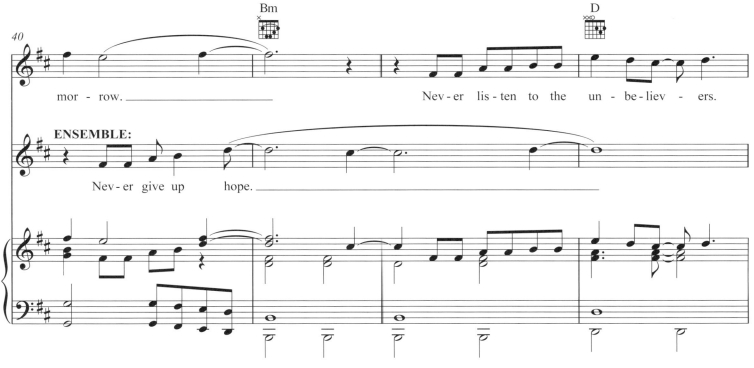

mor - row._____ Nev - er lis - ten to the un - be - liev - ers.

ENSEMBLE: Nev - er give up hope._____

You'll take ___ your falls, you'll hit ___ your ___ walls. Don't give in to

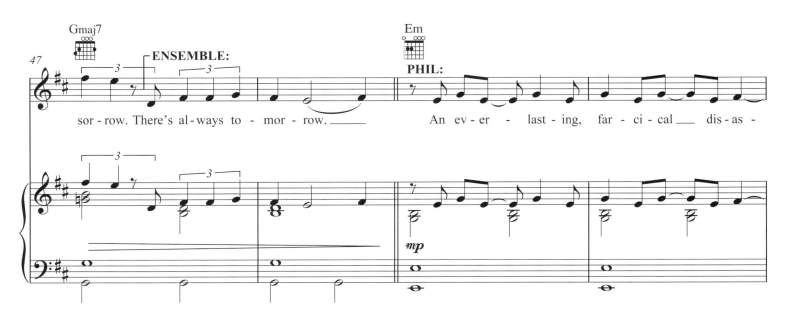

sor - row. There's al - ways to - mor - row._____ **ENSEMBLE:** **PHIL:** An ev - er - last - ing, far - ci - cal ___ dis - as -

up - on the path you have to tread. And in your head that lead - en dread.

The fuck - ing roads have all been trod. And there's no way and there's no God.

And God, oh God, this god - damn weath - er will last for - ev - er. But you must

ENSEMBLE:

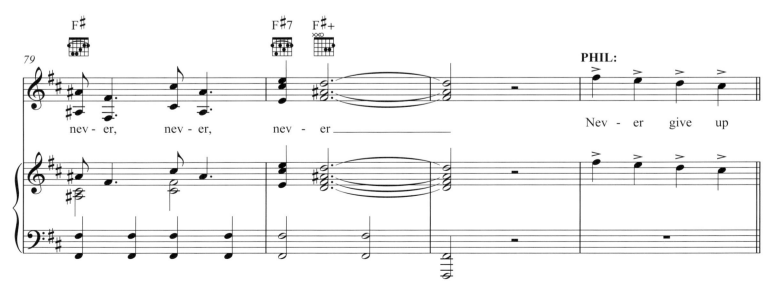

nev - er, nev - er, nev - er

PHIL:

Nev - er give up

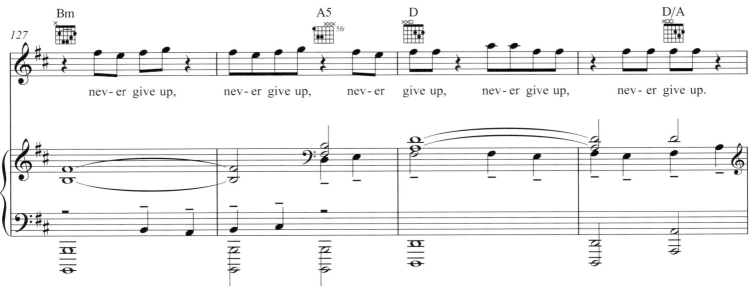

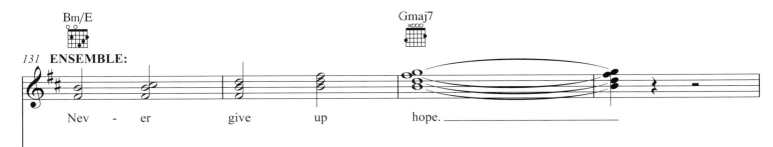

EVERYTHING ABOUT YOU

Words and Music by
TIM MINCHIN

mom,   or walk-ing your dog,   who you named Ste - ven,   be cause...   Well,

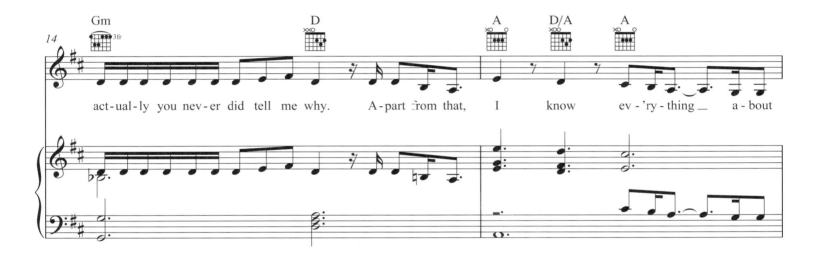

act - ual - ly you nev - er did tell me why.   A - part from that,   I   know   ev - 'ry - thing __ a - bout

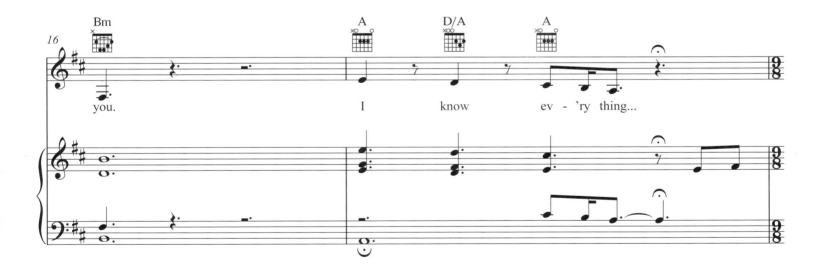

you.   I   know   ev - 'ry thing...

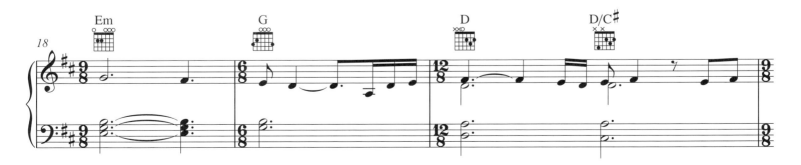

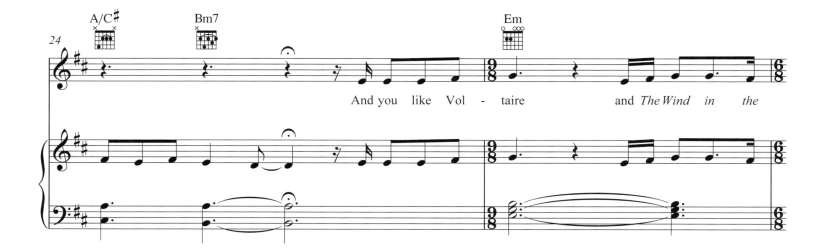

And you like Vol - taire and *The Wind in the*

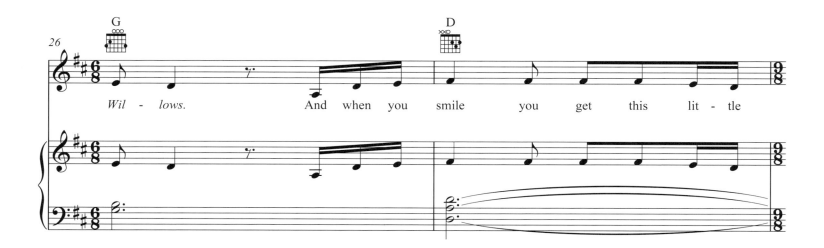

Wil - lows. And when you smile you get this lit - tle

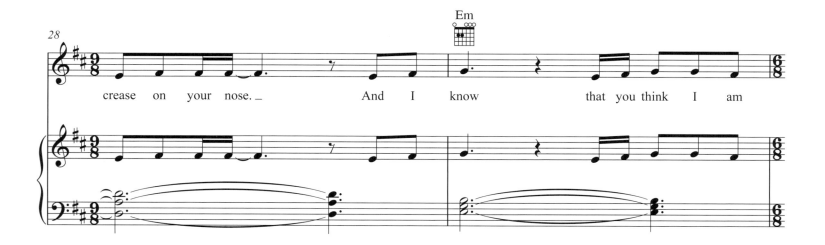

crease on your nose. __ And I know that you think I am

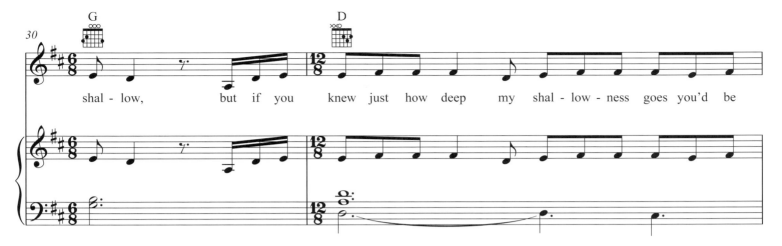

shal - low, but if you knew just how deep my shal - low - ness goes you'd be

shocked. And your toes go numb 'cause you wear in - ap - pro - pri - ate

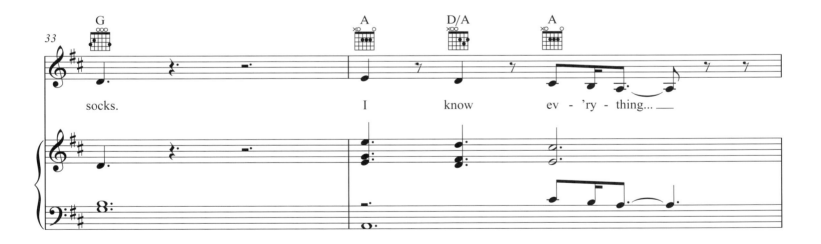

socks. I know ev - 'ry - thing... ____

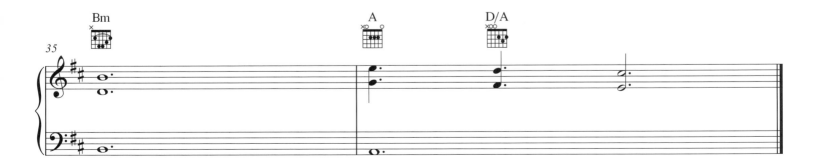

IF I HAD MY TIME AGAIN

Words and Music by
TIM MINCHIN

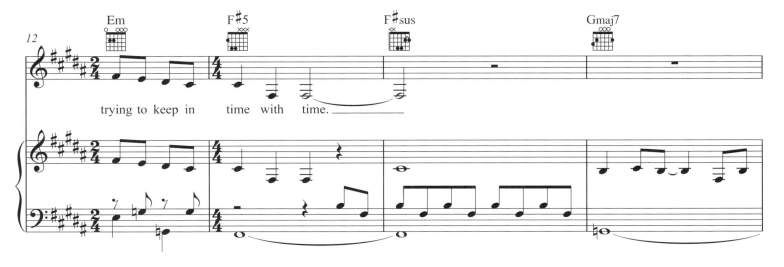

trying to keep in time with time._____

But if I could stop the clock for just one day...

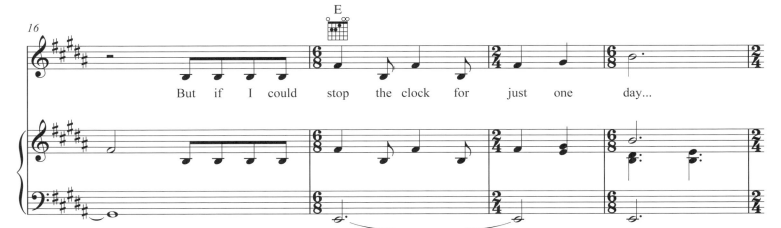

If I could freeze a mo - ment for a mo - ment, (a) rest be - fore the

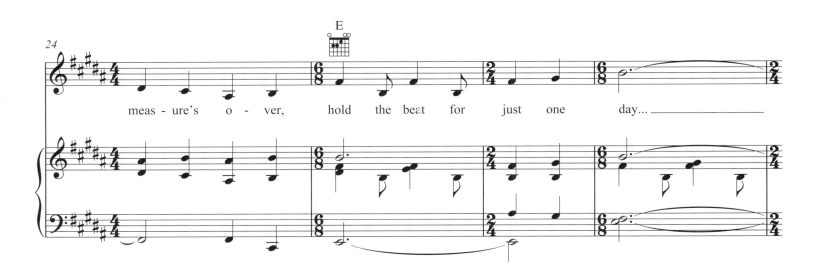

meas - ure's o - ver, hold the beat for just one day..._____

If I could wind it back and __ start a - fresh. __ Just a day to

catch my breath, to make mis - takes and set them right, de - lay the com - ing

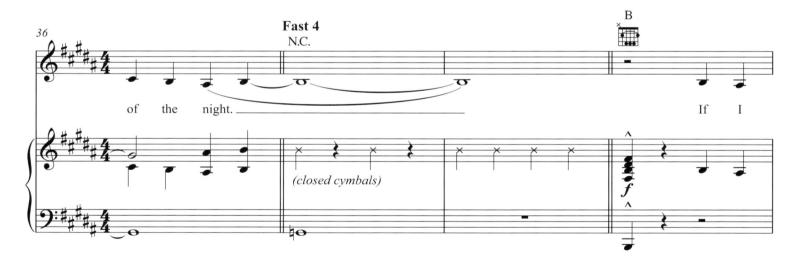

of the night. _____ If I

had my time a - gain __ I would do it all the same, they say, but

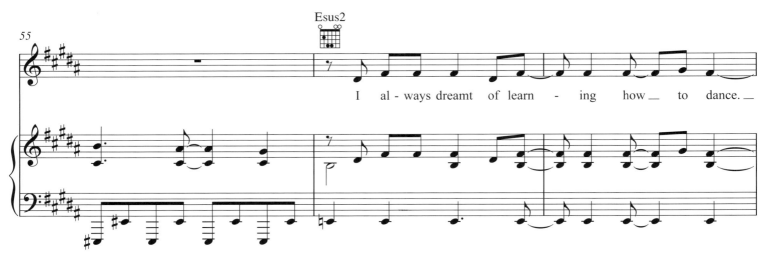

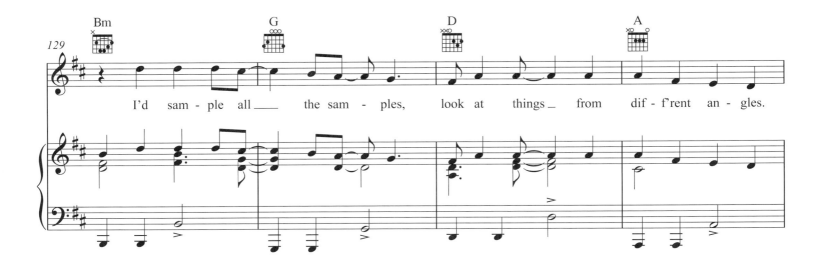

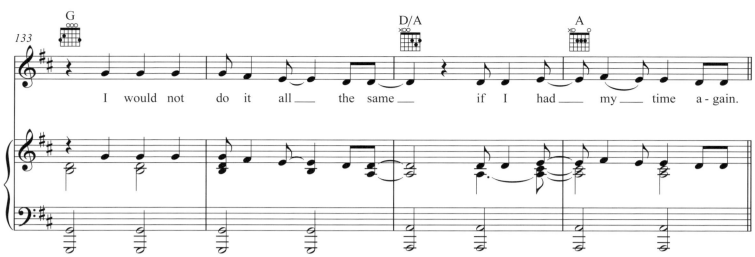

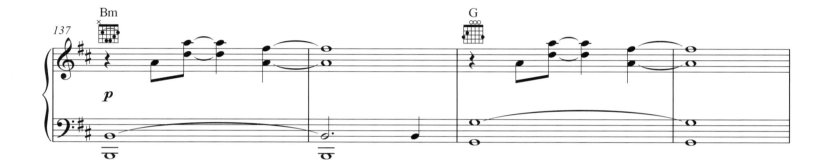

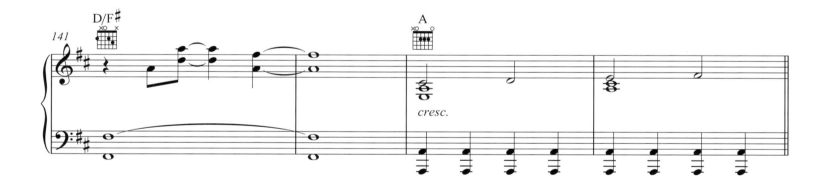

the things _ I'd han - dle bet - ter... I would send _ my un - sent let - ters.

If I _____ had ___ my _

PHIL:

I have start - ed sev - en hun - dred fights. And if you knew the end - less nights

(feeling of 4)

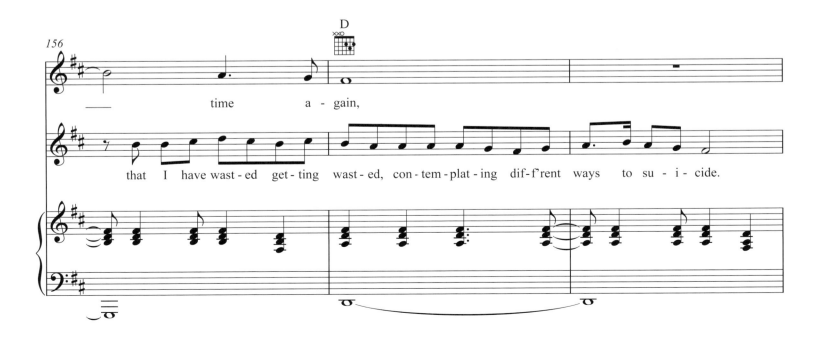

___ time a - gain,

that I have wast - ed get - ting wast - ed, con - tem - plat - ing dif - f'rent ways to su - i - cide.

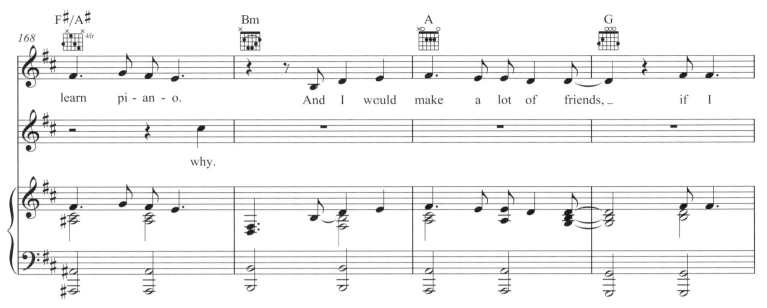

learn pi-an-o. And I would make a lot of friends, _ if I

why.

had my time... _ If I had my time a-gain, _

I had my time a-gain. _

ff (half-time feel)

_ I'd o-pen all the doors _ I

And I've _____ o-pened all the doors _ you

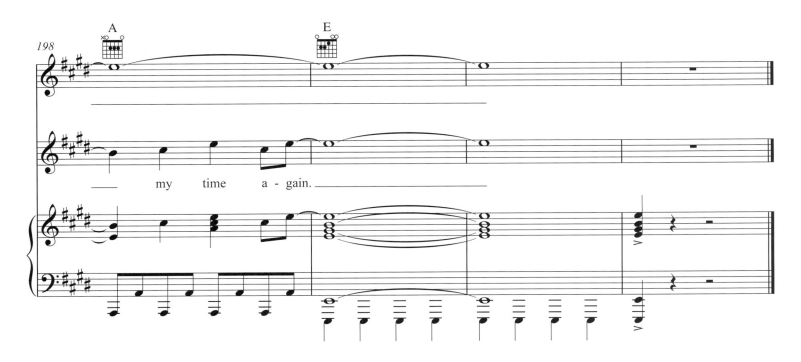

NIGHT WILL COME

Words and Music by
TIM MINCHIN

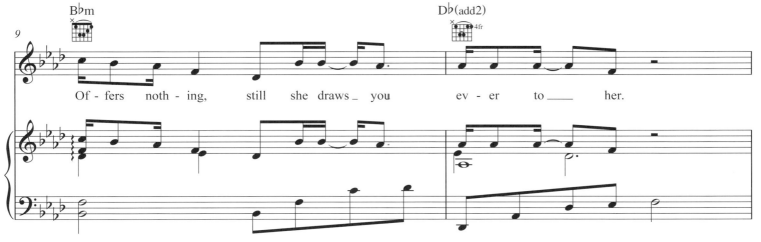

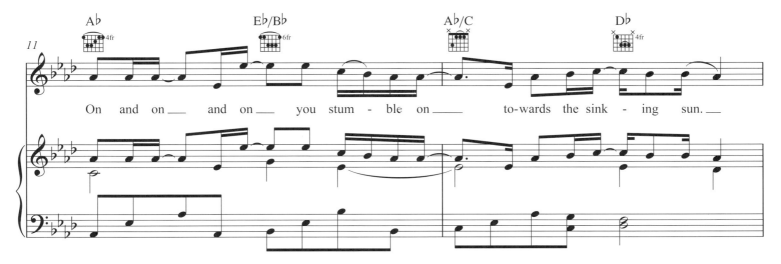

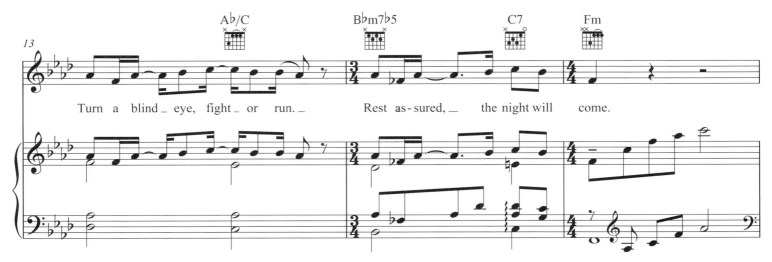

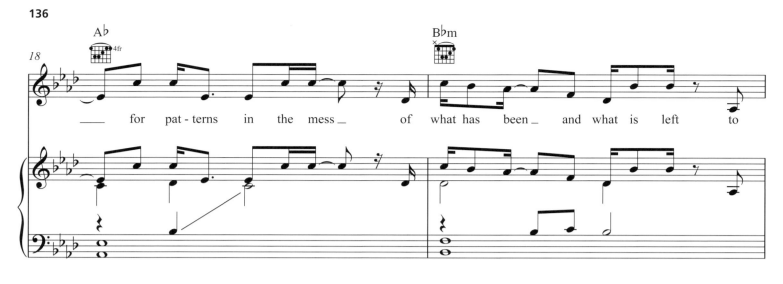

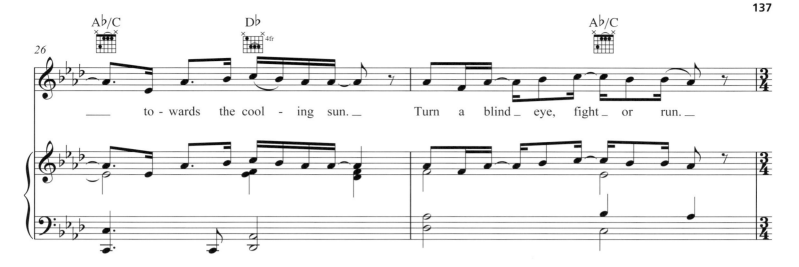

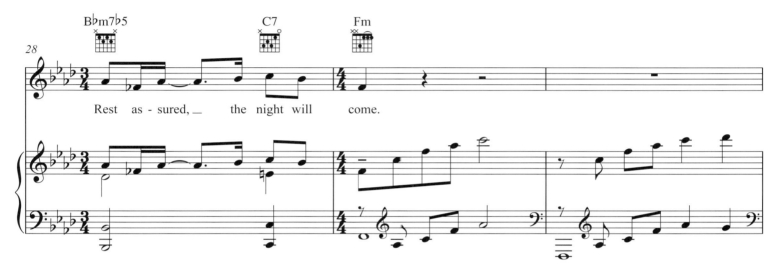

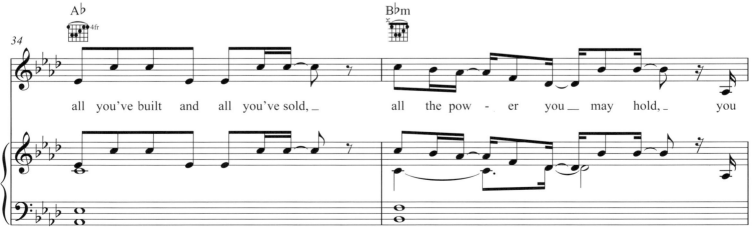

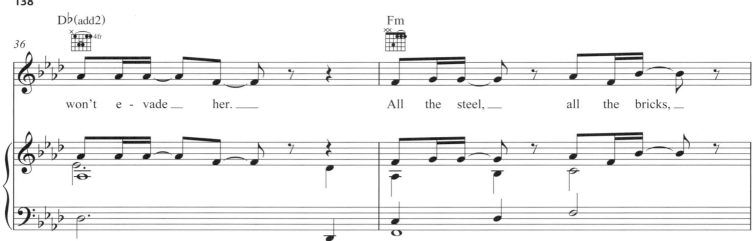

won't e-vade __ her. __ All the steel, __ all the bricks, __

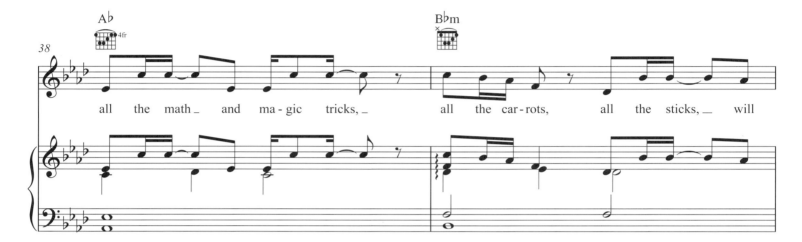

all the math __ and ma-gic tricks, __ all the car-rots, all the sticks, __ will

not dis-suade her. __ On and on __ and on __ you stum-ble on __

__ to-wards the fad-ing sun. __ Turn a blind __ eye, fight __ or run. __

Rest as-sured, _ the night will come. Rest as-sured, _ the night will

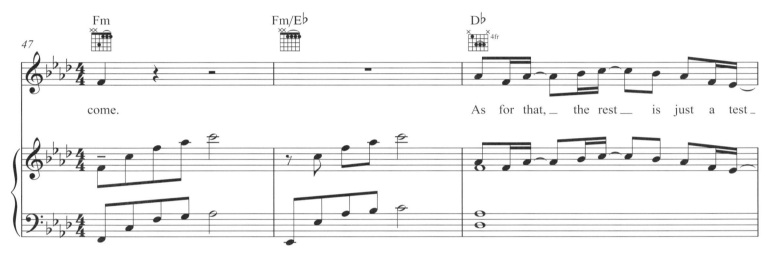

come. As for that, _ the rest _ is just a test _

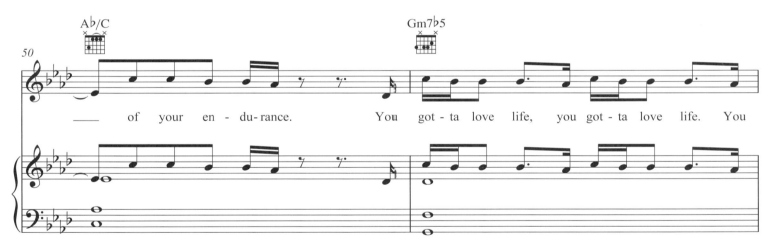

_ of your en-du-rance. You got-ta love life, you got-ta love life. You

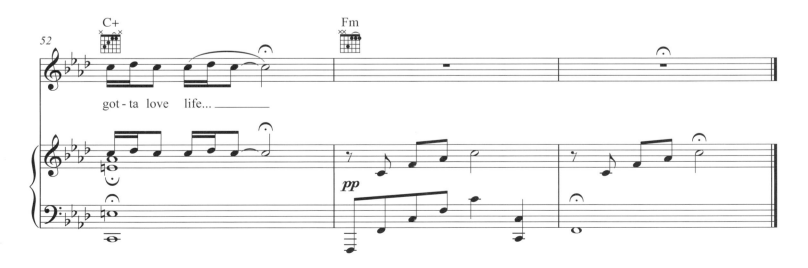

got-ta love life... _

SEEING YOU

Words and Music by
TIM MINCHIN

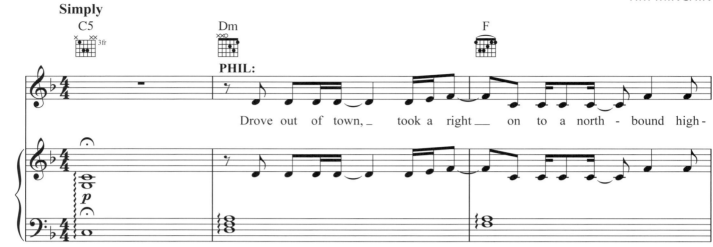

PHIL:

Drove out of town,__ took a right__ on to a north-bound high-

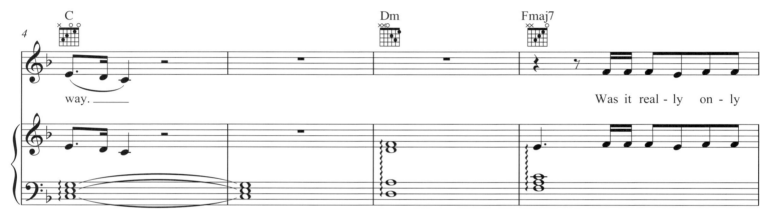

way.___ Was it real-ly on-ly

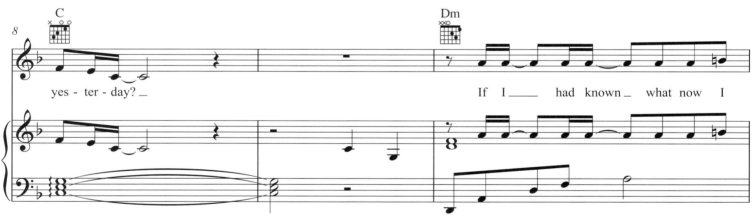

yes-ter-day?__ If I__ had known__ what now I

know, may-be I_____ would have tak-en a mo-ment,

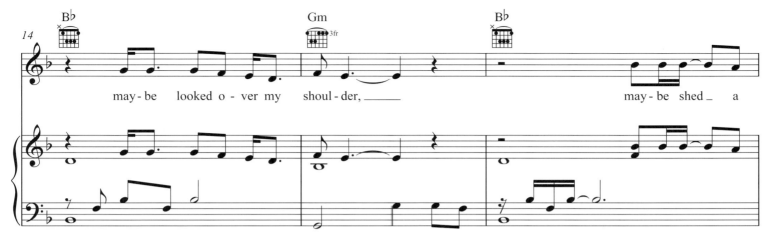

may-be looked o-ver my shoul-der, _____ may-be shed _ a

tear... Now I'm _____ here.

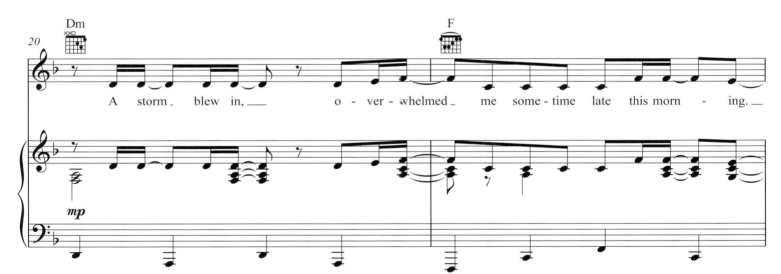

A storm _ blew in, ___ o-ver-whelmed _ me some-time late this morn - ing. _

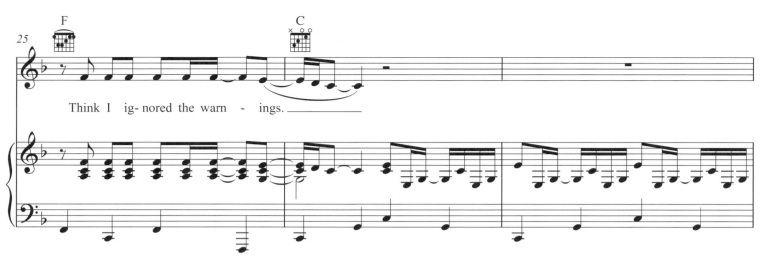

Think I ig-nored the warn - ings. _____

I've spent a life - time seek-ing signs, ___ read - ing lines, _____

try'ng to fore - cast ___ the fu - ture.

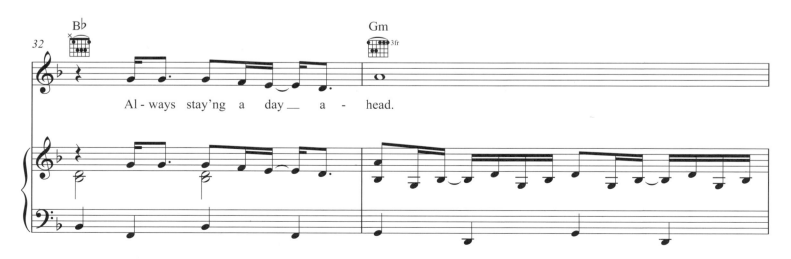

Al - ways stay'ng a day ___ a - head.

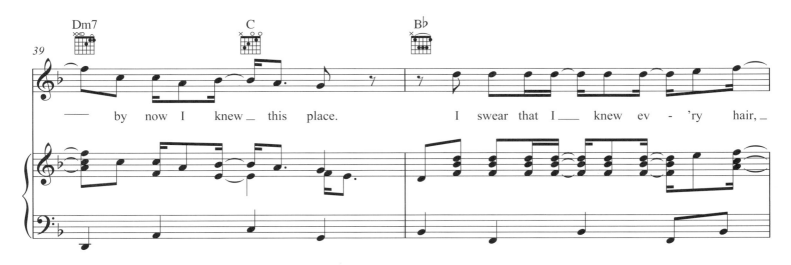

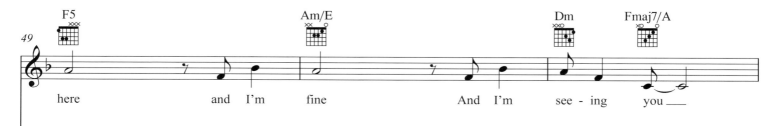

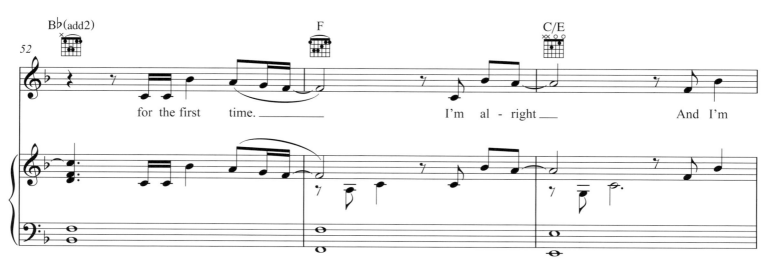

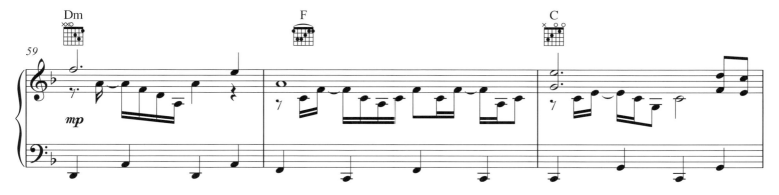

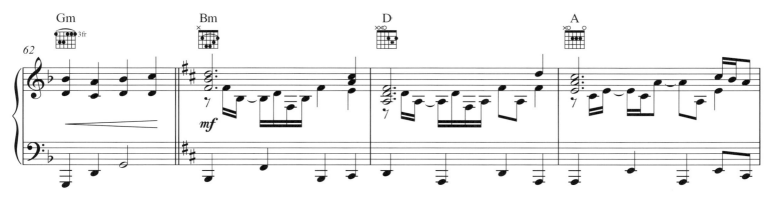

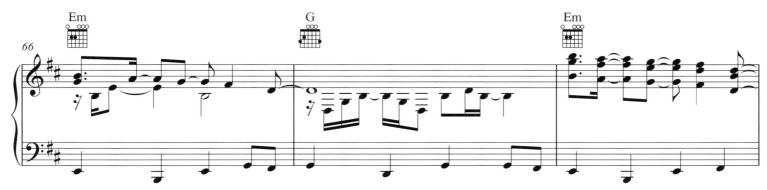

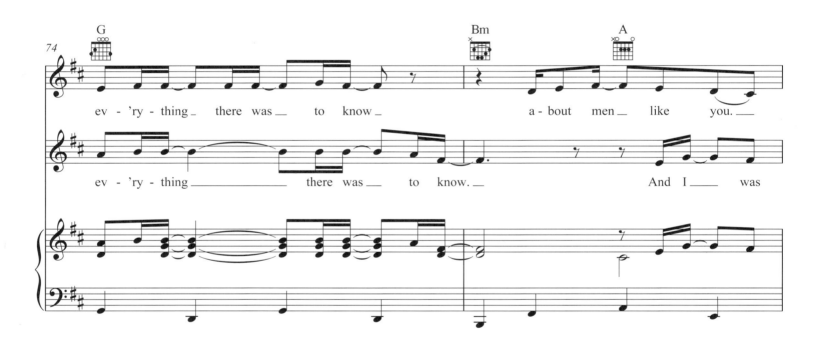

147

see-ing   you _____

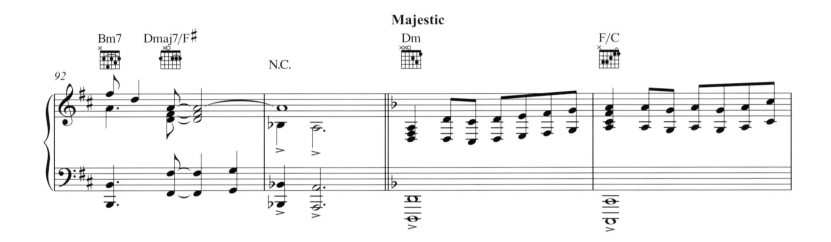

Majestic

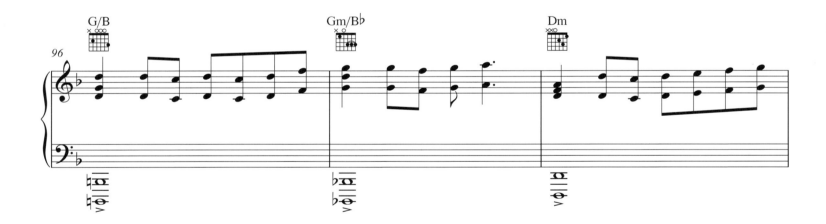

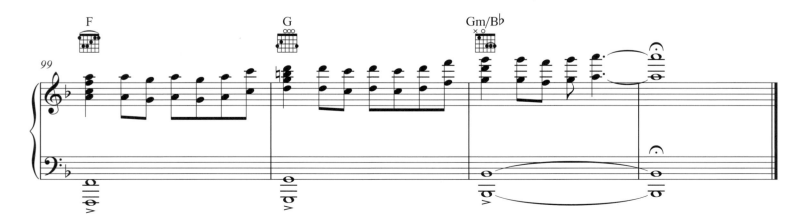